LAB MANUAL TO ACCOMPANY

AN INTRODUCTION TO
COMPUTER SCIENCE & PROGRAMMING

BY WALTER SAVITCH

THIRD EDITION

GREG DOBBINS

PEARSON
Prentice Hall

Upper Saddle River, New Jersey 07458

Vice President and Editorial Director, ECS: *Marcia J. Horton*
Publisher: *Alan R. Apt*
Associate Editor: *Toni Dianne Holm*
Editorial Assistant: *Patrick Lindner*
Vice President and Director of Production and Manufacturing, ESM: *David W. Riccardi*
Executive Managing Editor: *Vince O'Brien*
Managing Editor: *Camille Trentacoste*
Production Editor: *Mary C. Massey*
Director of Creative Services: *Paul Belfanti*
Creative Director: *Carole Anson*
Manufacturing Buyer: *Ilene Kahn*
Director of Creative Services: *Paul Belfanti*
Cover Designer: *Daniel Sandin*
Executive Marketing Manager: *Pamela Hersperger*
Marketing Assistant: *Barrie Reinhold*

© 2004 Pearson Education, Inc.
Pearson Prentice Hall
Pearson Education, Inc.
Upper Saddle River, NJ 07458

Pearson Prentice Hall® is a trademark of Pearson Education, Inc.
Java™ is a trademark of Sun Microsystems, Inc.

Printed in the United States of America

10 9 8 7 6 5 4 3 2 1

ISBN: 0-13-142233-2

Pearson Education Ltd., *London*
Pearson Education Australia Pty. Ltd., *Sydney*
Pearson Education Singapore, Pte. Ltd.
Pearson Education North Asia Ltd., *Hong Kong*
Pearson Education Canada, Inc., *Toronto*
Pearson Educación de Mexico, S.A. de C.V.
Pearson Education—Japan, *Tokyo*
Pearson Education Malaysia, Pte. Ltd.

Pearson Education, Inc., *Upper Saddle River, New Jersey*

CONTENTS

INTRODUCTION

This laborabory manual supplements the text *Java: An Introduction to Computer Science & Programming* by Walter Savitch. The text has 942 pages. The intent of this manual is to minimize the number of additional pages of text a student must read while providing structured learn-by-doing activities to reinforce the material presented in the text.

Although instructors may find other uses for this manual, it is designed with certain assumptions. It is not a stand-alone manual. The relevant text material for each laboratory should be covered in class at a time near but before the laboratory is given. The laboratory is assumed to be a closed, instructor-led lab. During most of the lab, the students will be developing a program using a computer.

Hence the purpose of this laboratory manual is to provide hands-on experience under the direction of an instructor in applying the concepts covered in the text. It is assumed the lab will have a format something like the following: the instructor or teaching assistant gives a short introduction explaining the background and programming problem and some related examples. The instructor in charge of the weekly lectures has made some reference to this lab activity for the week and perhaps also included some preparatory examples and illustrations in the lectures. Students in the lab have access to and can use a computer in the lab to complete the assignment. It is assumed that whereas the lecture may involve several hundred students, the lab involves groups of 25 or less each sitting in front of a computer to do work.

The student population most likely will be a varied mix of backgrounds and abilities, but this laboratory manual is written for the majority of students who are assumed to be "average" college students.

Each lab has a statement of purpose, objectives, and material from the text to review, but the heart of each lab is at least one programming exercise to be completed during the lab period, which is assumed to be 1 hour 50 minutes. or approximately this amount of time.

In this manual, practical industry experience is called on in the time available to point out good software engineering practices and to relate work situations the students will likely incur on the job. These include principles in requirements gathering, design and testing and quality assurance. In the two Graphical User Interface labs, we stress the importance of usability and discuss ways of understanding what this means in the customer's view.

Developing high-quality software is extremely important as is attested to by the following display due to the Faulkner Information Services.

Business	Cost per hour of downtime
Brokerage	$6.45 Million
Credit Card Sales Authorization	$2.6 Million
Home Catalog Sales	$90,000
Airline Reservations	$89,000
Tele-Ticket Sales	$69,000
ATM Fees	$14, 500

Permission for use granted by Faulkner Information Services.

We emphasize the importance of quality in software development and getting it right the first time. If a software defect is caught early in the development process then the cost is small compared to cost at final test before general customer availability. If a defect makes it through to the customer, then this often results in degraded performance and downtime. The preceding table shows the range of consequences of downtime in terms of cost per hour for various business sectors.

This lab manual is integrated with the text. There should be a multiplier effect as the material herein interacts with the material in the text.

The labs have the following format.

LABORATORY Number	Title

OVERVIEW

A high-level summary of the lab activity.

We try to tie in our real world experiences and bring some practical applications of the ideas where possible in classroom. The beginning section (as well as other sections) often has some material with this theme.

OBJECTIVES

Here we outline what the lab will accomplish.

PRELAB PRACTICE QUIZ

In most labs, you will have a quiz based on topics covered in the lecture and ideas you will need to do the lab. (In the interest of using existing resources and integrating materials, sometimes a quiz item is similar or identical to a Self Test question in the text.) Alternatively, the instructor may wish to give material from these quizzes at the end of a lecture as an attendance quiz once per week when the material for the chapter has been covered and it is time for a lab. The author has used this latter approach in teaching large lecturer sections and then used the scores as a quiz average in the final grade. It is often hard to take attendance in a lecture class with 150 students. This is also a way of encouraging and taking attendance. If a student ends up on the boundary between a B and a C at the end of the semester then the instructor can take a look at the attendance quizzes to make a decision. Another variant is to give quizzes not every week but four or five randomly scattered over the semester or quarter.

TEXT REFERENCE

Here we mention relevant text material that will help you do the lab. The lab in turn will reinforce these key concepts. From time to time we will also use other facts in the programs that represent prerequisites for knowing how to do the lab.

Some labs require you to read Java documentation at http://www.sun.com as practice for work on the job which will rarely involve reading a textbook. Instead you will have to glean information from many sources working in a team situation and integrate it with some ingenuity into a solution.

There also may be a few questions or exercises to help you study and get ready for the lab.

The rest of the format has to do with the actual programming that you will do in the lab session. This usually follows the format below.

The heart of the material in each lab is the section on programming exercises.

PROGRAMMING EXERCISES

Programming exercises include a description of the problem to be solved or the program to be developed during the lab session. Like real-world problems, there is no consistent format used for presentation of the problem although we stress the importance of understanding requirements and the importance of involving the customer in development projects.

Most labs have a section on testing. Several formats are suggested and sample test cases given to get you started testing your program. There is usually a section on testing program behavior.

Testing Program Behavior

Suggestions as to how or what to test are given in most cases. Several labs have a more formal approach where a test case format is used. Following is a more formal approach showing a section of a table giving test cases from Laboratory 5.

Inputs			Expected Output		Observed Output	Test Status
Quiz Average	Midterm	Final	Final Average	Grade		
89.5	100	99	96.875	A		Pass
89.5	100	-45	User notified of invalid input and prompted to re-enter this item. Program continues.		Same	Pass
0.0	0.0	0.0	0.0	F	Same	Pass
100	100	100	100.0	A	Same	Pass

It is noted how metrics for communication can be developed in the workplace from this king of information. Examples are percent tests passed and percent tests complete—need to know information in a schedule-driven work environment such as the students will soon experience!

Finally, there is a section on screen shots.

Screen Shots of Program Behavior

This section gives you an idea what your final result should look like. Sometimes various views of the program behavior is given. Below is an example from Laboratory 14 on GUIs with menus.

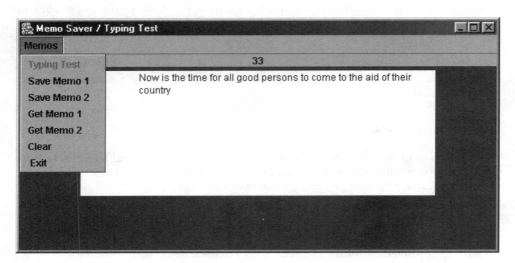

In this laboratory, you will add a typing test to a menu example given in the text. The timer is at 33 seconds to go in the test. A bell will ring at time = 0. Note also that if the menu is accessed during the test, the menu item in use is disabled.

There are fourteen laboratory sessions in this manual. Generally, the labs parallel the text with one lab per chapter. However, there are several notable exceptions. Chapter 9, "File I/O" has two labs: one for text file I/O and one for binary file I/O. There are labs at present for Chapter 11 "Recursion" and Chapter 13, "Applets and HTML." There are two labs for Chapter 12, "Dynamic Data Structures": one for vectors and one for linked lists.

Generally, the labs become longer and more detailed as you become more experienced. If you want to see some short labs look at labs 1, 2 and 3. If you want to see longer labs, look at labs 12, 13 and 14.

ACKNOWLEDGMENTS

The framework of this material developed over a period of three years 2000 – 2003 teaching large classes of 150 – 300 students at The University of South Carolina using the text by Walter Savitch. During this time, my head teaching assistants were Len Bowers, Antonio Rodriguez and Taraka Peddireddy, who assisted in developing the basic topics and some of the programs. Over this time, we used all three editions of the Savitch text.

Dr. Fred Druseikis helped to get the lab manual done in a short time during summer 2003. Fred was particularly helpful when a programming solution was detailed and needed in a short time. Dr. Druseikis and I worked a combined total of over 35 years at NCR and AT&T. This helped in adding a practical, business aspect to the manual. Dr. Duncan Clarke, who also spent some industry time at AT&T graciously volunteered to proofread the manual and made a number of valuable suggestions and corrections.

Dr. Robert Cannon was responsible for getting a Java course started early at the University of South Carolina in the late 1990s. He helped me to begin teaching the course in Fall semester 2000 by providing advice and helpful materials.

All errors or inaccuracies that remain are mine.

Greg Dobbins
Columbia, SC
Summer 2003

OVERVIEW

In this laboratory exercise, you will learn specifics about the organization of computer systems from a programming perspective. This is the first step on the road to becoming a software developer. Software developers need to have a good view of the capabilities of a system to program it effectively. This often requires a somewhat deeper knowledge of the system's capabilities than other kinds of end users are expected to know. This knowledge can be gained from course work and practical experience. This lab and the rest of this lab manual are a start in that direction.

In this lab, we are going to gain some first-hand experience so that you can use the Java language and the TextPad editor effectively with the Microsoft Windows operating system running on your personal computer. Throughout this book we will be using the combination of Microsoft Windows (98/ME/2000/XP) and Sun Microsystem's Java 2 Software Developer's Kit (SDK).

One of the best ways to learn Java is to learn it using the "minimal" environment required to run a program. In this lab, we will be using the minimal environment approach because this knowledge will be directly transferable to other software platforms you may encounter during your career. The details of other systems will be different, but the way the processes and procedures are organized will be very similar, if not identical.

Sun's Java 2 SDK is designed to be *platform independent*, meaning that it can be run on platforms of many vendors. Platform independence does not come easily. It needs to be designed into the software from the beginning. This is one of the distinguishing characteristics of Java.

There are two major types of computing platforms in the commercial market place today: *proprietary systems*, such as Microsoft Windows, various vendor-branded versions of the Unix™ systems (for example, Sun's Solaris, or SCO's SVR4), and other operating systems such as VMS, System/390, Mac OS X, and so forth; and *open systems* such as BeOS, Amiga, BSD Unix and its variants, and GNU/Linux. Modern operating systems share many common features and have to address all of the issues of operating systems theory; the distinction between proprietary and open source has to do with licensing of systems for commercial and other uses.

Platform independence assumes that a software developer is familiar with a specific native platform (for example, Microsoft Windows) and can follow the instructions for successfully installing the SDK on his or her platform. We'll go through the setup process in this lab.

There is a paradox to becoming a software developer: On the one hand, a software developer creates software that has new capabilities and in doing so must come to understand everything about his or her creation; on the other hand, systems today are so complex that it is impossible to know the details of how everything actually works. Most of software development is about how to balance the need to understand something about everything and everything about something.

By working through this lab you should be able to set up the Java 2 SDK on any PC to which you have access. If you are taking a course, there may be computers already configured with the required software.

TEXT REFERENCE

This lab assumes that Chapter 1 has been covered in the lecture and you have read it. You should specifically review Section 1.3, "A Sip of Java," focusing on the sample program in Display 1.5 and the subsections "Compiling a Java Program or Class" and "Running a Java Program." The self-test questions throughout the book are a great way to test your understanding and to prepare for labs and tests! Here are a couple with their numbers from the text to ready you for this lab.

1. Suppose you define a class named SuperClass in a file. What name should the file have? _____.

2. Suppose you compile the class SuperClass. What will be the name of the file with the resulting bytecode? _____.

The answers to these questions are on page 35 of the text.

Self-test questions occur throughout the text and are good to test your understanding of concepts as you go along through the book. First pretend it is an actual test and try to do the problem without looking at the answer. Answers are at the end of each chapter in an area called "Answers to Self-Test Questions."

OBJECTIVES OF THIS LAB

The objective of this first lab is to become familiar with your lab environment and with compiling and running Java programs in the different settings. Lab environments will vary from location to location, as will how your instructor wants to do things in the lab. Hence, these are a set of recommended activities that your instructor may alter or do differently.

In this lab, you will learn

- How to create a Java program and run it in a command-line window
- How to use the TextPad editor
- Some basic facts about the Java system running under Windows
- Some pointers on how to install the Java 2 SDK

This lab should also give you idea how to set up a Java environment on your home computer. If you are taking a course, the environment will probably be set up for you already. Since there are differences from one operating system to the next, we do not undertake a complete set of instructions.

MATERIALS YOU WILL NEED

Of course, you will need a personal computer running Microsoft Windows 98/ME/2000/XP. Practically speaking, the minimum recommended configuration for Windows will be adequate for the needs of this course.

The CD-ROM provided with the text contains the Java 2 SDK Release 1.4.0 and the TextPad editor. These two packages comprise a simple but functional "development environment" for Java. A development environment typically includes a set of tools that make common tasks encountered during software development easier. Examples of such tasks include creating and editing program text, running programs, and debugging programs.

A more sophisticated development environment is also on the CD, the Sun ONE Studio 4 *integrated development environment* (or IDE). (In the past, Sun ONE Studio was named Forte for Java.) One of the features of this IDE is to support source code control (sharing programs between developers on the same project) and the design of graphical user interfaces. We won't use Sun ONE Studio 4 in this book.

At the root of almost all development environments is a tool that helps you edit programs. TextPad is such an editor. It is a programmer's editor because it has features that make it easier to deal with program text rather than ordinary English text. You should contrast the features of TextPad with those of the standard Windows tools Notepad and Wordpad. (For example, try editing a simple Java program in Notepad and TextPad.) You can develop Java programs with any editor, and there are several leading alternatives (such as the emacs and vi editors.) In addition to text editing, in TextPad you can easily type or paste in Java programs, compile them, and run them. In a business or software development setting, a more elaborate environment is often needed.

If you have access to the Internet, you can download the most recent versions of these programs. The download for Java 2 is about 38 MB, so it will take a long time unless you have a high-bandwidth connection. The download for TextPad is about 1.6 MB. Most likely both are already installed on your lab computer and you may not need to concern yourself with the details of installation.

You can find out if Sun's Java 2 SDK has been installed on your computer in one of two ways:

1. In the Windows Control Panel, go to "Add/Remove Programs" and look for Java 2 SDK among the listed applications.
2. Alternatively, look for the required installed files in a directory containing the letter "J2SDK" as part of its name, such as C:\J2SDK1.4.0_02.

If you find only the Java runtime environment (JRE) installed, you need to add the SDK. The JRE contains only the runtime environment, not the development tools. The primary functional difference between the JRE and the SDK is that the JRE only contains the Java interpreter (the Java Virtual Machine, or JVM); the SDK contains both the Java *interpreter* and the Java *compiler*. Hence you can run programs in the JRE, but you cannot compile or debug them.

The examples in this manual are geared to Java 2 SDK Release 1.4.0; earlier releases may have bugs or other limitations for more advanced examples later in this manual. You should avoid using very old versions of Java—for example, the JVM distributed by Microsoft has significant limitations.

You can access the Java 2 SDK from Sun's Web site, http://java.sun.com, and TextPad from http://www.textpad.com.

Note: Both the Java 2 SDK (and other components and tools collections from Sun generally) and Textpad editor have licensing agreements that limit your ability to use or distribute their product in all cases. Further, TextPad is a shareware program whose continued support and development is funded by voluntary contributions of its users.

EXERCISE 1   COMPILING AND RUNNING A JAVA PROGRAM WITH TEXTPAD

To do this exercise you will need to have access to a computer with the TextPad editor and the Java 2 SDK already installed. You should know how to run Windows programs using menus and the mouse.

Preparation

Visit http://www.textpad.com.

Review the FAQ at http://www.textpad.com/support/faq/index.html.

You may also find the TIPS file at http://www.textpad.com/support/tips/index.html useful after you have gained some experience with the tool.

1. Verify that you have TextPad installed; you can install Textpad either from your textbook CD or by downloading it from the Internet.

2. Access the source code on your text CD and make a copy of the sample Java program shown in Display 1.5 on page 23 of the text. This program is in **E:\Source_code\ch01\FirstProgram.java** (assuming your CD is mapped as the "E" drive.) You can make a copy of a file by using the File Cut and Paste operations in Windows Explorer, or Internet Explorer. Copy the first_Program.java from the E: drive to a parallel file hiereachy on the C: drive.

3. Bring up TextPad by going to the Windows Start button, "Programs" menu and select TextPad.

4. Open the file **C:\Source_code\ch01\FirstProgram.java** in TextPad.

5. On the TextPad menu bar, select Tools—Compile Java. If there is a compilation error, then you will be notified. If you do not copy the file from your CD drive to the hard disk but try instead to open the file on the CD drive, an error you might get is if the compilation took place in a directory in which you do not have write permission. Remember, the result of the compilation is a file; in this case, FirstProgram.class. Visit the directory **C:\Source_code\ch01** and check that this file is there.

6. Next, on the Menu Bar of TextPad, click on Tools and then double click on "Run Java Application". This action should run the program. A DOS Window should open, letting you see the output of the program. Virtually all of the Java programs we will write run from a "DOS-BOX". To dispose of the DOS Window, click on the window "X" and then when the message box window appears click "Yes".

7. In the program, edit the first line and replace the word "FirstProgram" with "firstExample". (That is, change the name of the class.) Compile the program. You should get a compilation error.

8. Why do you get a compilation error?

9. Remember to change the name back to "FirstProgram".

EXERCISE 2   COMPILING AND RUNNING A JAVA PROGRAM
WITH TEXTPAD

1. As a second exercise with TextPad first open up TextPad from the Programs list using the "Start" button. Then load the program from TextPad by using the "File" button on the menu bar. Do File—Open and then find FirstProgram.java in whatever directory you have it and double click on it. This should bring the program into the editor window. Compile and run the program as before.

2. You can put in comments by using // for a single line comment and "/* */" for a multiline comment. "/*" must go first, then the comment, and then */.

3. You can disable any line in the program by typing "//" at the very start of that line. Try disabling certain lines in the program and see what happens. "//" turns a line of code into a comment. The compiler treats this as documentation and otherwise ignores it. Hence, it neither checks it for syntax errors nor generates executable bytecodes for it.

One good way to learn about programming is to do as students do in other fields such as literature and mathematics—study good examples. In programming there is another feature to the learning by study of examples: You can experiment and make changes and see what happens.

All the source code that appears in your text book in the Displays is on your text CD. Make good use of it!

EXERCISE 3   WHAT'S IN THE JAVA 2 SDK?

The SDK consists of several pieces:

1. A directory structure
2. A set of environment variables describing where important files can be found
3. Programs or software tools that perform specific, well defined functions
4. Software components that can be used by other programs that you develop
5. Documentation
6. Working examples

The JAVA_HOME environment variable names the root directory for the Java 2 SDK. Relative to the JAVA_HOME directory, the following subdiretories are important:

- Bin
- Demo
- Lib
- JRE
- Include

The **Bin** directory contains the tool programs. The **Lib** directory contains the JAR files (acronym: Java ARchive) that can be used in creating other programs. The **JRE** directory contains the runtime (only) environment. The **Include** directory contains C-language declarations for linking programs with the JVM. The **Demo** directory contains interesting examples of Java programming. Most of these programs are "applets" that must be run under a Web browser.

A JAR (acronym: Java ARchive) file is a file that contains other files in a directory hierarchy. A JAR file can be read by the JVM during execution of a program as a source of the implementations of classes required by the program.

A second environment variable, the CLASSPATH, is sometimes required, especially when using programs developed in earlier versions of Java. The CLASSPATH lists explicitly the names of possible directories or JAR files that the JVM should search when trying to locate a class during execution.

Questions for Review

1. What is the full path to the Java interpreter on your computer?
2. What is the full path to the Java compiler on your computer?
3. Find and run the applet named Nervous Text.

OVERVIEW

In this laboratory exercise, you will review concepts from Chapter 2 in the text and then write several short Java programs to gain Java programming experience and reinforce these concepts.

The knowledge of the basics of running a Java program is essential to all other programming in Java. The simplest programs are linear consisting of executing program statements in order one after another and then program termination. An important topic in Chapter 2 is primitive data types and performing arithmetic calculations with these different data types.

Chapter 2 introduces the main data types available in Java and the special String class. You will get practice in using methods from the String class.

Statistics is a subject that increasingly involves the interests and efforts of businesspeople. The subject of Statistics applies mathematical methods to the collection and analysis of data to support decisions in many areas. Examples are decisions that need to be made with regard to

- Whether a certain type customer is a credit risk
- Analysis of large amounts of banking transaction data for patterns that would indicate fraud
- Determining an estimate for the average time to failure for a product such as a PC or a type of tire with a new tread design

To have a level of certainty in providing answers to decision makers about such issues, statisticians have to collect data, usually referred to a sample. This activity must be done in a certain manner, takes time, and costs money. Hence, in business, an important question is, how large a sample size do we need to be reasonably certain of our analysis and the answer we give decision makers? To do this, you need to do sample size calculations. Your first lab exercise involves a sample size calculation. Be careful to apply data typing and arithmetic operations in the correct order.

OBJECTIVES

Write Java programs to become familiar with and learn about

- Basic program structure and data types
- Arithmetic operations
- The Class string
- Creating objects in Java
- Basics of documentation and style

TEXT REFERENCE

This lab assumes that Chapter 2 has been covered in the lecture. The student should specifically review these topics from Chapter 2 before attempting Lab 2:

- Primitive types and assignment statements
- Type casting
- Arithmetic operators
- The class String and String methods
- Documentation and Style

PRELAB PRACTICE QUIZ

In each sentence, fill in the blanks with appropriate answers or supply a word that makes the sentence correct.

1. The _____ operator is used to connect two strings to make one longer string.

2. To include a double quote inside a character string, you must use a(n) _____ character.

3. Every variable in Java must be _____ before it is used.

4. The value of 48% 10 is _____.

5. Give the declaration for a Java variable called index of type int as it would appear as a line of code in a program. The variable should be initialized to zero in the declaration.

   _____.

6. Suppose we have this statement in a program:

   ```
   char value ='a' ;
   ```

   Write a line of code that will convert the character stored in "value" to its ASCII code integer value and store it in a new variable "N".

   _____.

7. What is the output produced by this code?

   _____

   ```
   double result;
   result = (2 / 3 ) * 3;
   System.out.println( "(2 / 3 ) * 3 equals " + result );
   ```

PROGRAMMING EXERCISES

1. **Statistical Sampling and Estimation of Population Parameters**

    Frequently, in business or scientific research, a certain population is of interest and it is desired to estimate a particular parameter or characteristic of the population to a certain accuracy and to be confident that this estimate is correct. Examples are

    *   The average or mean life of a product such as a new brand of light bulb touted to be extra long lasting or a new laptop computer
    *   The average amount owed by Americans on credit cards
    *   The average distance from home for students at a certain large university

    In each instance, we have certain common factors and conditions. There is a population of interest, a particular numeric constant that we would like to know, and a certain obvious impracticality in getting the answer exactly. Usually, this impracticality involves time and money or some sort of cost. In many such cases, statistical sampling provides an answer to this dilemma.

    To use statistical sampling, we need the following information:

    E = the error that is tolerable in the estimate of the population parameter
    Z = 1.96 a statistical factor associated with 95% confidence in estimations.
    σ = population standard deviation, a factor having to do with the spread or scatter in the population values. A value that may be used for σ involves estimated largest and smallest values in the total population. Let M be an estimate of the largest value observable in the population and m an estimate of the smallest value in the population of interest; then substitute $\sigma = (M - m)/4$.

    The sample size, N, that will be necessary to estimate the population average with 95% confidence is given by the following formula:

    $$N = ((Z * \sigma) / E)^2$$

    Programming Requirements

    Assume that you have been given the job of estimating the average age of students at your university or college. Your method is randomly to select N names from the university phone listings and ask the person's age and then compute the average age from this sample of N names. According to statistical theory, this method should have an approximate 95% chance of getting within E of the true average population age. Think of a reasonable estimate of M and m for your university and use those values to estimate σ in the preceding formula.

    Your program should accept M, m, and B as estimates from the keyboard and the program output should be the correct value of N expressed as an integer value that is rounded up. The value of $Z = 1.96$ should be stored in the program. Store it as a named constant using the directions given in Section 2.4, "Documentation and Style," in the text. There should be some text message such as "The sample size to use is" and then give the computed value for N.

Put a comment at the beginning of your program to identify the name of the program and the date. The following is a screen shot of a correctly running program:

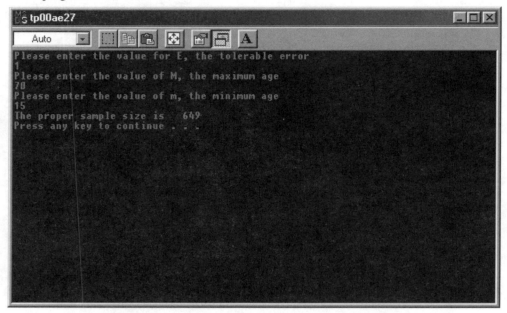

2. **Exploring Appendix 3 Unicode Character Set**

This exercise should acquaint you with some of the material in the appendices of the text. In particular, you will learn about how the computer takes the information you enter in at the keyboard and how the computer stores and begins to process this information.

Programming Requirements

Write a program to check out the Unicode Character Set table given in Appendix 3 of the text. Your program should ask the user to input a keyboard character from the list given in Appendix 3 and then output the integer ASCII code for this character.

3. **Working with Strings**

Think about input from the keyboard. It comes in as strings of characters. Often you want just one part of a string or you want to put a particular string with another string. In Java, Strings are a kind of class type, and as you will soon learn, classes have methods or ways of manipulating data from members of the class. This will begin to acquaint you to the new way of thinking about programs in terms of classes and objects.

Programming Requirements

Write a program to accept two strings, S1 and S2, as input from the keyboard. Create a new string S3 as the concatenation of the first two strings with a space separating them and output S3. The program should have this output:

S1 length of S1
S2 length of S2
S3 length of S3

S1 and S2 should print out as they were entered. For S3, the part that is due to S2 should be in UPPERCASE. The following is a screen shot of a correctly running program:

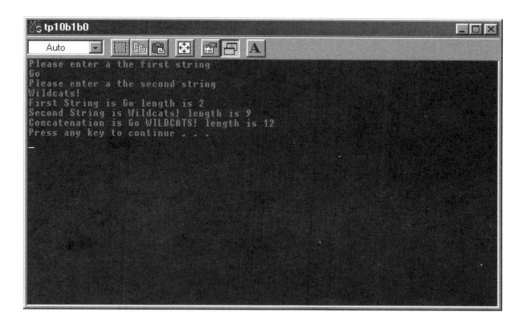

ANSWERS TO THE PRELAB PRACTICE QUIZ

1. + or Concatenation

2. Escape

3. initialized

4. 8

5. int index = 0;

6. int N = (int) value;

7. = 0*(2/3)*3 equal 0

OVERVIEW

In this laboratory exercise, you will review concepts from Chapter 3 in the text and then write several short Java programs to gain programming experience that reinforces these concepts.   The programming exercises will use the looping constructs in different ways. You will need to know how to use Boolean variables to control the program flow. Some of the programming will involve manipulation of String variables.

OBJECTIVES

Write Java programs to become familiar with and learn about

- Use of some of the String methods from Chapter 2 (see text page 71)
- Branching statements
- Java loop statements including nested for-loops
- Programming with loops
- the type Boolean

TEXT REFERENCE

This lab assumes that Chapter 3 has been covered in the lecture.   The student should specifically review these topics from Chapter 3 before attempting Lab 3. Also review the class String and the String methods in Chapter 2, particularly the "equals" method and the methods for extracting a substring from a string. Be sure and study "if-else", "multibranch if-else", the switch statement, and compound Boolean statements with operators !, ||, and &&. Review also the use of nested loops and where they are necessary.

PRELAB PRACTICE QUIZ

In each sentence, fill in the blanks with appropriate answers or supply a word that makes the sentence correct.

1. An ! in an expression means _____ of a Boolean value.

2. A case label is used with a(n) _____ statement.

3. Java has two forms of multiway branches: the _____ and the

    multibranch _____ statement.

4. The most common kinds of loop bugs are unintended _____

    loops and _____ loops.

5. What output is produced by the following statements?

    ```
    System.out.println( true && false);
    ```

    _____

    ```
    System.out.println( true || (x ==0));
    ```

    _____

6. What is the output produced by the following code fragment?

    ```
    String value1 = " Lab 3";
    String value2 = " lab 3";
    if (value1.equals((value2))
            System.out.println(" The values are equal");
    System.out.println("End");
    ```

    _____

7. What will be the value of w after the following section of code executes?

    ```
    int w = 4, q = 6;
    if (q > 5)
       if (w == 7)
            w = 3;
       else
            w = 2;
    else
       if (w > 3)
            w = 1;
       else
            w = 0;
    ```

    Answer is _____.

PROGRAMMING EXERCISES

1.   String Subsetting and Classification

Often data are not available in the exact form needed. It is necessary to extract from the data the information that we want and then proceed with the processing of this data. Sometime this takes the form of classifying the data into different types and then performing some operation on the data. The first program involves this type of situation.

Program Requirements

Write a program that will allow the user to input a 10 digit telephone number with hyphens following the area code and prefix. Your program should check the input for proper length and position of hyphens. The program should have this behavior. If area code is

- 606, then print "Hello, Kentucky"
- 312, then print "Hello, Chicagoland"
- 803, then print "Hello, South Carolina"
- Any other area code then print "Hello, may I help you?"

Screen Shot of Program Behavior

Here is a sample of how the program should respond to various inputs.

Testing Program Behavior

You should always test the program using test cases. This can be done by planning the test cases and their results with a table such as the following:

Case #	Input	Expected	Observed	Status
1	606 345-7898	Prompt to redo	Prompt to redo	Pass
2	803-777-9593	Hello, South Carolina	Hello, South Carolina	Pass
3	8803-777-9593			
4	703-			
5	123 999 9000			
6	34-777-9593			
7				
8				
9				

It is a good idea in testing to test things that are "close to the boundary." These occur in the preceding example when you have one too many numbers or not quite enough numbers or one missing "-", etc. The number of cases that can be thought of for this simple program illustrates the problem of assuring software quality. Test cases are said to have good coverage if they tend to "cover" or be representative of the type of errors that can occur.

2. Print a Triangle

Write a program that will print out an equilateral triangle shape.

Program Requirements

Your program should accept a positive integer N, say, for example, 5 is the value you enter, and print out a triangle with apex to the right and an altitude equal to $N=5$ "+" characters printed horizontally.

```
+
++
+++
++++
+++++
++++
+++
++
+
```

Screen Shot

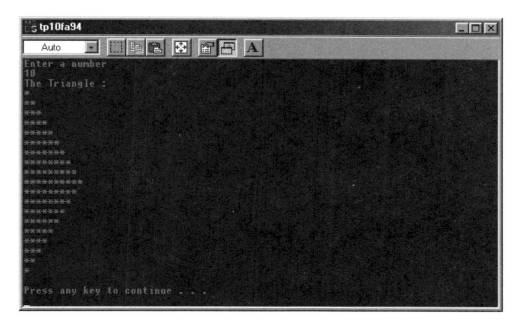

ANSWERS TO THE PRELAB PRACTICE QUIZ

1. negation

2. switch

3. if-else and switch

4. infinite and off by one

5. false, true due to the short circuit rule

6. End

7. 2

OVERVIEW

In this laboratory exercise, you will review Java class concepts from Chapter 4 in the text and then write a Java class definition and driver program to test this class. The programming exercise will use programming techniques developed in the text.

OBJECTIVES

Write Java programs to become familiar with and learn about

- Java class definition, file naming and compilation
  - instance variables
  - methods and their types
- Instantiating an object of a class and testing or using this object in a separate program

TEXT REFERENCE

This lab assumes that Chapter 4 has been covered in the lecture. The student should specifically review topics from Chapter 4 before attempting this. These topics include the following:

Class Name and Definition
Class definition and naming the class and the .java file that it is stored in. Remember that when you define a class, the name must begin with a capital letter and the class definition must be stored in a file with the same name and extension ".java". Example: class name is "Automobile" and the class definition is stored in a file "Automobile.java".

Class Instance Variables and Methods
Review the class "Automobile" example in the text. The declaration of instance variable, such as "fuel" and "speed", is according to a certain format and must appear in the class definition file as follows:

```
private double fuel;
private double speed;
etc.
```

Be sure to read the section in the text on "public" and "private" modifiers beginning on page 214 of the text.

Methods must show their return type in their declarations and the parameters that are required to use the method. If the method does not return any value, then this is indicated by the word "void". Examples of method declarations are

```
public void increaseSpeed( double howHardPress);
```

```
public double readAmountFuel( );

public double setAmountFuel(double fuel);
```

Read about the types of methods. This begins on page 189 in the text. Notice that two of the aforementioned methods return a value and one does not. Which methods are "mutators" and which are "accessors"?

Review "return statements", blocks, and local variables.

PRELAB PRACTICE QUIZ

In each sentence, fill in the blanks with appropriate answers or supply a word that makes the sentence correct.

2. A(n) _____ is an action that a Java object can perform.

3. A case label is used with a(n) _____ statement.

4. A(n) _____ is a piece of information passed to a method.

5. Which of the following is a class type?
   int   double char   String

6. An equals(. . .) method has a (n)_____ return type.

7. If you see code such as " this.name", what does "this" mean?

   _____

8. A variable declared within a method is called a _____ variable.

9. _____ means that the data and the actions are combined into a single item (a class object) and that the details of the implementation are hidden.

10. Suppose that you have a class called Turtle. Write a line of code that will create a Turtle object.

    _____.

11. Name two methods of the Math class in Java.

    _____ and   _____

PROGRAMMING EXERCISES

1. The Triangle

    In this exercise you will define a class called Triangle. The lengths of the sides should be positive integers in this exercise. In the second, exercise you will change this to double.

    Use the "new" keyword to instantiate a triangle object. In the second programming exercise, we will use a more complete method referred to as a "constructor".

    The data needed for the class will be the data necessary to specify a general triangle in terms of the lengths of its sides, which should be expressed as integers. These data will be stored in the instance variables of the triangle object.

    The method of triangle object instantiation using "new" does not allow for initialization of data values. New obtains a memory location for the address of the object and creates the instance variables but does not initialize them. A helpful text reference is on page 234, under "FAQ: What's new?". Instance variables can be assigned values in the program. For this program, allow values to be input from the console for the instance variables and then assigned. The best way to do this is with "set" methods. So have set methods for each side and also "get" methods to read out to the screen current values. Good examples can be found beginning with page 240 of the text with the "Species" class.

    Additionally, create methods to calculate properties of a triangle, such as the perimeter, and to determine if it is a right triangle. You can determine if it is a right triangle by checking if $A^2 + B^2 = C^2$, where A, B, and C are the side lengths in some assignment such that the equality holds. That is, it is a right triangle if given the values set for the sides, you can find two sides such that the sum of their squares equals the square of the other side. One specific example is a triangle such that $A = 3$, $B = 4$, and $C = 5$.

Screen Shot of Program Behavior

    Here is a sample of how the program should respond to various inputs. Your job is to write a program that does this.

Test your program for faulty behavior. Try values that are close to the boundary and try unusual combinations of side lengths. The following table provides some examples. Complete the table with other test cases.

A	B	C	Error Conditions?	Right Triangle?	Perimeter	New A	Right Triangle?
4	4	5	No	No	13	3	Yes
1	1	10	No				
1	1	1	No				

Even if we are not math majors, with a little thought, the second test tells us that something is wrong. Our program is working, but it is not checking very carefully about what is or is not a triangle. If we draw a triangle with base equal to 10 and two other sides of length equal to 1, then we would have found a shorter way to get from one end of the base to the other that was not a straight line! So we need to do more checking. We will do this in the next exercise.

2.   The TriangleSecondTry

Enhance the preceding Triangle class by allowing instance variables to be of type double and by adding

- A constructor. The constructor should accept three nonnegative double parameters.

- A way of detecting if this is a valid triangle or not.

- A method to calculate the area of a Triangle object using Heron's formula. For this you will need the square root static method (sqrt ( )) from the Math class introduced in Chapter 5, page 279–280.

    Heron's formula states that for any triangle with sides having lengths equal to A, B, and C,

    Area = sqrt($S * (S - A) * (S - B) * (S - C)$),   where

    $S = (A + B + C)/2$ or the perimeter divided by 2.

    You will note that for Heron's formula to work that each factor has to be non-negative. If for instance,

    $S - A < 0$,   then

    $(A + B + C)/2 - A < 0$ and this is equivalent to

    $A + B + C < 2*A$ or $B + C < A$.

    Hence, to avoid problems and have a triangle that is a triangle, you need to be sure that $B + C \geq A$ for all assignments of side values to A, B, C. This is the check step that you must build into your program!

Screen Shot of Program Behavior

Here is a sample of how the program should respond to various inputs. So your job is to write a program that does this.

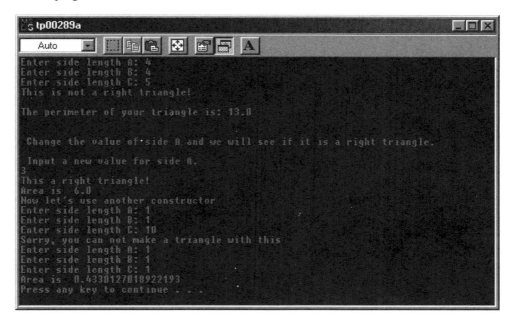

ANSWERS TO THE PRELAB PRACTICE QUIZ

1. method

2. switch

3. argument

4. String

5. Boolean

6. "this" refers to the current object referenced and this object has an instance variable called "name".

7. local

8. encapsulation

9. `Turtle Harvey = new Turtle( );`

10. rand( ) and sqrt( ), for example

LABORATORY 5

Classes, Objects, and Methods

OVERVIEW

In this laboratory exercise, you will learn about using classes in programs to do work. You will make decisions about data and data types to use, what methods to use, and how they should interact with themselves and the data or instance variables of the class.

The programming exercise is a "what if" program for computing your final grade given a record so far in the course and possible future grades. In business, sometimes one wants to do a "what if" analysis to see how things are going to work if certain future conditions prevail.

OBJECTIVES

Write Java programs to continue to become familiar with and learn about

- Java class definition, file naming, and compilation
  - instance variables,
  - methods and their types
- Instantiating an object of a class and testing or using this object in a separate program

TEXT REFERENCE

In this laboratory exercise, you will review Java class concepts from Chapter 5 in the text and then complete exercises to reinforce these concepts.

PRELAB PRACTICE QUIZ

In each sentence, fill in the blanks with appropriate answers or supply a word that makes the sentence correct.

1. If a method definition is labeled _____, then that method can be invoked using the class name rather than the object name.

2. Every primitive has an _____ _____ that serves as a class version of that primitive type.

3. A(n) _____ is a class method that is called when you create an object of the class using new.

4. You can form a _____ of class definitions you use frequently. You can then use the classes in any program without needing to move them to the same directory as the program.

5. If a class is named Student then every _____ for that class must also be named Student.

6. Suppose you want to make a class a member of the package named mytools.lib. What do you need to put in the file containing the class definition?

    _____

    Where does this statement go in the class definition?

    _____

7. List the instance variables methods in SavitchIn and draw a Unified Modeling Language (UML) class diagram of SavitchIn.

PROGRAMMING EXERCISES

What Would My Grade Be If . . .

OBJECTIVES OF THIS PROGRAMMING EXERCISE

List the instance variables, methods in SavitchIn. Draw a UML class diagram of SavitchIn.

Write a program to become familiar with and learn about

The concepts of a class and an object that instantiates the class
Information hiding and encapsulation
How to define classes in Java
Creating objects in Java
The concept of a reference in order to understand class variable and parameters

SCENARIO

You are taking a computer science class and in reading the syllabus you see that the instructor has the following method of evaluation:

A. There is a quiz average based on 100 points.
B. There is one midterm exam and one final exam, each graded on the basis of 100 points.
C. The final exam counts 50%, the midterm counts 25%, and the quiz average score counts 25%. It should be converted to a percent before they are graded.

The grading scale is as follows based on the final average:

Grade	Final Average (FA) in this Range
A	≥90
B	≥80 but < 90
C	≥ 70 but < 80
D	≥ 60 but < 70
F	< 60

You would like to write a program so that throughout the course you may enter the grades you have earned thus far and then do some "what if" analysis. For example, you may have these grades so far:

Quiz   8 Pts.
Midterm   80 Pts.

You want to see in this case what sort of grade you would get if you score a 98 on the final. Or you may want to suppose it is the end of the semester, put in all your grades, and then check to see what your letter grade would be on the University grade report.

REQUIREMENTS AND PLANNING

Think about the way this program should behave. Normally, on the job, you write a program because you have a customer who specifies what work the program should do and then your job is to meet or exceed the customer's expectation. So to make your task more specific and clearer, let us require that this program accept as input:

```
Student Name
Quiz Grade
Midterm Score
Final Score
```

This program should output the letter grade based on the aforementioned input.

How does this problem relate to Chapter 4 in the text? How can we use classes and methods here?

_____

How many classes do you think you should have? _____

What data do you need and what types should each data item be? What do you call these data items in Java?

_____

How many methods should you have in each class? What should they be?

_____

Produce a solution to the preceding program requirements using these steps.

1. Define a class called StudentGrade.java
2. Include instance variables for the data required. These data include
   Student name
   Quiz, Midterm, Final and Overall Average
   Letter Grade for the course based on above data

3. The class should have the following input and output methods:
   inputName()—reads the name of the student from the console.
   printName()—prints the name of the student to the console.
   inputQuiz()—reads the quiz score from the console.
   printQuiz()—prints the quiz score to the console.
   InputMidterm—reads the midterm score from the console.
   printMidterm—prints the midterm score to the console.
   InputFinal—reads the final score from the console.
   printFinal—prints the final score to the console.
   printOverallScore()—prints the overall score to the console.
   PrintLetterGrade()—prints the letter grade to the console.
   InputRecord()—reads the entire student record to compute the numeric score and final letter grade. This method reads the name, quiz, midterm, and final exam. Use helper methods.

Note: All scores input into the program must be checked that they are in the range 0 to 100 inclusive. If not, user must be prompted that data is invalid and given opportunity to re enter. Program continues until valid data has been entered for all inputs.

4. The class should have the following computing methods:
   ComputerOverallScore()—computes the overall score.
   ComputeLetterGrade()—computes the letter grade.

5. Test your class with StudentGradeTest.java, which reads a student record, computes the overall score and letter grade, and prints the record. It makes use of all the aforementioned methods in StudentGrade.java, so make sure you write all the methods.

The code for StudentGradeTest.java is as follows:

```java
public class StudentGradeTest
{
        public static void main(String args[])
        {
                StudentGrade studentgrade = new StudentGrade();
                /**
                 * reads the student record , should
                 *      -       prompt for the username
                 *      -       prompt for the quiz score
                 *      -       prompt for the midterm score
                 *      -       prompt for the final exam score
                 */
                studentgrade.readRecord();

                //computes the letter grade
                studentgrade.computeLetterGrade();

                /**
                 * prints the student record
                 *      - prints the student name
                 *      - prints the quiz score
                 *      - prints the midterm score
                 *      - prints the final exam score
                 *      - prints the overall score
                 *      - prints the letter grade
                 */
                studentgrade.printRecord();

        }

}
```

UML

Complete the following UML diagram for the class StudentGrade above.

StudentGrade
-   name: String
+ inputName( ): void

SOME PRELIMINARY DESIGN WORK

Fill in the following table for the data types that you need.

Instance Variable	Data Type
Name	
Quiz	
midtermExam	
finalExam	
overallScore	
letterGrade	

Given the form of the tester program, which methods should be private helper methods and which methods should be public methods of the class?

_____.

What could go wrong with your program if your scores are integer variables and you enter a double value?

_____.

What is a database? How is your program like entering data into a database? How is it very different from this? In what aspect is it very different?

_____.

Screen Shot of Program Behavior

Here is a sample of how the program should respond to various inputs. Your job is to write a program that does this.

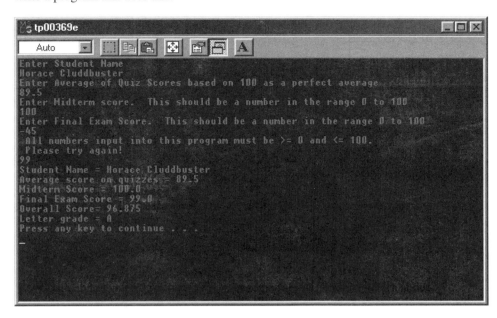

Testing Program Behavior

Test your program for faulty behavior. Try values that are close to the boundary, and try unusual combinations of scores. Examples are shown in the following table. Complete the table with other test cases.

Inputs			Expected Output		Observed Output	Test Status
Quiz Average	Midterm	Final	Final Average	Grade		
89.5	100	99	96.875	A		Pass
89.5	100	–45	User notified of invalid input and prompted to re-enter this item. Program continues.		Same	Pass
0.0	0.0	0.0	0.0	F	Same	Pass
100	100	100	100.0	A	Same	Pass
and so carry on!						

In a real-world situation, you should be prepared to demonstrate that your test has high *coverage*. Coverage is a measure of the extent to which the test plan and cases cover all possible inputs to the program.

A person who does this activity of testing is often in quality assurance and is called a QA tester. Often what the director of development or engineering will want to know from the QA department is the status of the testing. Common metrics are percent tests completed and percent tests passed. For the preceding data, these metrics would be 25% complete and 100% passed (assuming 12 tests in the plan.)

ANSWERS TO THE PRELAB PRACTICE QUIZ.

1. static

2. wrapper class

3. constructor

4. package

5. constructor

6. package mytools.lib;   Make it the first instruction statement in the file.

7. See UML examples in chapter and Appendix 4.

OVERVIEW

In this laboratory exercise, you will review Java class concepts from Chapter 6 in the text. There are two programming exercises. The first is short and is to write a Java class definition called ArrayMethods and driver program to test this class. The programming exercise will use programming techniques developed in the text and help you to understand the basics of defining, testing, and using arrays in programs. The second program is in three parts and involves sorting arrays. You will be given a test program and an implementation of the Selection Sort algorithm discussed in detail in the text. Your main job will be to implement another sort algorithm referred to in the text and known as Bubble Sort.

In the Business World

if you are developing software for customers, then of course the software must be as bug-free as possible and meet the customers' expectations for correctness and accuracy. In making the sale, one factor that is also very important is the performance of the software with respect to time. Generally, customers want software that scales well. "Scales well" here means that as the work load increases, then the customer wants to see proportionate increase in response time. So if a the software can do a workload of size X in $t = 100$ milliseconds and now a workload of size $2X$ is submitted, then customers tend to expect that this would take $2t$ or 200 milliseconds. This is linear scaling. The customer wants this response time to be reasonable and not slow down business transactions. We have included a section in the exercises where you can do a performance analysis of these two sort methods to see what the proportionate increase is for your computer with respect to workload.

Arrays are about storing data and manipulating the data to produce calculated values or some other result. Many programs require data as input but do not use arrays. Code for computing the average of a set of numerical values input from the keyboard follows. It is essentially the example given in the text on page 343, except that the number of values has been changed to a slightly larger number to make another point for why arrays are important.

```
int count;
double next, sum, average;
System.out.println("Enter 20 temperatures: ");
sum =0;
for (count =0; count < 20; count++)
{
      next = SavitchIn.readLineDouble( );
      sum = sum + next;
}

average = sum/20;
```

Now suppose you have your grades on the last 20 quizzes in a particular class. A short quiz is given every day by your instructor, and the possible points is 10. This program calculates the average, but suppose you also want a measure such as the spread or difference of these values from the average. In statistics, a measure called the sample standard deviation is used. You will learn about this in this lab exercise. In order to calculate the standard deviation, you must be able to subtract each value from the average and do some calculations with these values. In the preceding program, this type analysis is not possible because the orginal values are not available to be compared after the average is calculated. An array provides a way to keep the data in the program in an efficient manner and then use these data for further calculations later during the program.

In this lab you will create an array and use it to make calculations on data input to the array. We call this program ArrayMethods.

OBJECTIVES

Write Java programs to become familiar with and learn about

- Creating and accessing arrays
  - Array constructor
  - Initializing arrays

1. Using arrays
   2. Length instance variable
   3. Defining array methods to do statistical calculations such as the mean, minimum, maximum, and standard deviation of a set of numbers stored in the array
- Sorting arrays and analysis of algorithms
4. Bubble sort method
5. Selection sort method

TEXT REFERENCE

This lab assumes that Chapter 6 has been covered in the lecture. The student should specifically review topics from Chapter 6 before attempting this lab. These topics include those discussed in the Objectives.

Additionally, in this lab you will need to know how to calculate the maximum, minimum, average or mean value, and standard deviation of a set of numbers stored in an array. All but the last statistic are discussed in the text so we will explain the standard deviation.

Given a set of N numbers, $X_1, X_2, ..., X_n$ the sample standard deviation, s, of the numbers is defined as

$s = $ sqrt($\Sigma(X_i - X\text{bar})^2 / n - 1$) That is, the sample standard deviation is the square root of the sum of the squared deviations of each number X_i in the sample from the average value (Xbar), divided by $n - 1$ (the number of data items minus 1).

PRELAB PRACTICE QUIZ

1.   _____ is a single name for a collection of data of the same type.

2.   A method for sorting a list is _____.

3.   What will be the output produced by the following code?

```
int k;
int [ ] a = new int [10];
for ( k = 0; k < a.length; k++ )
a[ k ] = 5*k;
for ( k=0; k < a.length; k++)
      System.out.print( a[ k ] + "   ");
System.out.println( );
```

4.   Write a line of code using the "curly brackets" method to load these values:

97, 45, 100, 34, 42

into an integer array called "scores". Be sure to include a declaration of the array type.

5.   Study carefully the example of the Selection Sort beginning in the text with Section 6.4, "Sorting Arrays," page 383. Do the self-test questions on page 388 of the text. Read the description of the Bubble Sort on page 412 of the text.

Suppose we are given the array defined as follows:

```
int[ ] yourArray= { 5, 2, 1, 8, 4 }
```

Show the state of this array in each pass of the selection sort. Initially we have

5 2 1 8 4

After the first pass of the algorithm we have

2 1 5 4 8

Trace through all the steps until the algorithm terminates.

6.   Do the same exercise for Bubble Sort.

PROGRAMMING EXERCISES

1. Array Methods
   Download or obtain from your lab instructor the partially completed class *ArrayMethods.java*. This is a template for what you are to develop in this part of the lab. This template is shown here.

   This template class has a constructor that initializes an array intArray with a set of random integers in the mathematical interval (-1000, 1000). This means you need to generate random numbers like -42, 0, 234, -789, 999, -890, and so on. In order to do this, you will need to use the method rand( ) of the Java Math class. Usually a method like this generates random numbers in the range (0, 1) and you have to transform this to get the range of values that is desired. This is the reason for the following line of code:

   ```
   intArray[i] = (int) (Math.random()*2000.0 - 1000.0);
   ```

   The methods for finding the minimum, maximum, average, and standard deviation of the data set stored in the array are "stubbed in" in the template as minValue( ), maxValue( ), meanValue( ), and StandardDeviation( ). Recall from page 294 of the text that a "stub" is a simplified version of a method that is not good enough for the final class definition but is good enough for testing and is simple enough for you to be sure it is correct.

   The goal of this part of the lab is to complete this template and have a running program that computes the statistical values minimum, maximum, mean, and standard deviation from a randomly generated data stored in an array. To accomplish this you need to meet the programming requirements.

   Program Requirements

   - Complete the method minValue( ) so that it returns the minimum value in the array intArray.
   - Complete the method maxValue( ) so that it returns the maximum value in the array.
   - Modify the display method so that it neatly prints to the screen all the elements in the array.
   - Modify the method meanValue so that it computes and returns the mean value of the elements of intArray.
   - Complete the method standardDeviation( ) by using the preceding formula.
   - Write a main method to create an array and test each of the preceding methods.

```
/**
 * Class to test usage of standard array functions such as
 * min, max, and average.
 *
 *
 */

public class ArrayMethods
{
       private int[] intArray;

       /*********************************************
        * Constructor initializes the array with NUMINTS
random integers
        * ranging from -1000 to 1000.
        */

       public ArrayMethods()
       {
              intArray = new int[100];
              for (int i=0; i<intArray.length; i++)
              {
                     intArray[i] = (int)
(Math.random()*2000.0 - 1000.0);
              }
       }

       /*********************************************
        * Calculate and return the minimum value of the array
        * @return minimum value in the array
        */
       public int minValue ()
       {
              return 0;       // provide implementation.
       } // end minValue

       /*********************************************
        * Calculate and return the maximum value of the array
        * @return maximum value in the array
        */
       public int maxValue ()
       {
              return 0;       // provide implementation.

       } // end maxValue
       /*********************************************
        * Calculate and return the mean value of the array
        * @return mean value of the elements in the array
        */
       public double meanValue()
       {
              return 0;       // provide implementation.

       }//end meanValue

       /*********************************************
        * Calculate and return the standard deviation of the
array
        * @return standard deviation of the elements in the
array
        */
       public double standardDeviation()
       {
              return 0;       // provide implementation.
```

```
}//end standardDeviation

/*********************************************
 * Display all of the values in the array.
 */
public void display ()
{
                // provide implementation.

} // end display

//Tester for this class
public static void main(String[] args)
{
        //Be sure to include calls to test all the
        above methods here
}

} // ArrayMethods
```

2. A Longer Programming Exercise: Selection Sort/Bubble Sort Performance Comparison

The goal of this exercise is to do a performance comparison between the Selection Sort and Bubble Sort Algorithms implemented in Java. The Selection Sort Algorithm is featured in Section 6.4, "Sorting Arrays," beginning on page 383 of the text and is discussed in detail. The Bubble Sort algorithm begins on page 411 in the text but is not discussed in any detail. Detail on the Bubble Sort is supplied in what follows.

First carefully review the Selection Sort and Bubble Sort algorithms given in text.

The goal of this lab is to implement the Bubble Sort algorithm in a Java Class. The Selection Sort class and a Test Program will essentially be available as downloads or in some other way from your instructor. The greatest effort in this lab is on the Bubble Sort class and then making it work with the Selection Sort and Test classes.

Sorting is essentially a CPU/memory bound operation. (CPU = Central processing unit.) For this reason, if you run the program for this lab on different machines with slow, medium, and fast processors, then a positive linear relationship will be observed between the time to complete the sort and the MHz of the processor.

Bubble Sort

The Bubble Sort algorithm goes through all adjacent pairs of elements in the array from the beginning to the end and interchanges any two elements that are out of order. This brings the array closer to being sorted. The procedure is repeated until the array is sorted. It's called Bubble Sort because it is as if the "lighter" numbers float to the top (beginning) of the array and the "heavier" numbers sink to the bottom(end).

The following pseudocode outlines the method of the Bubble Sort.

1.   Start from the beginning of the array (index = 0).
2.   Compare the value in the array with the one at the next highest index. If it is greater (than next highest), then swap their values. If not, then do nothing with these two values.
3.   Increase the index (index++) and do Step 2.
4.   If you did at least one swap in this pass through the array, then start at again at Step 1. Otherwise, the array is sorted in ascending order.

Use this pseudocode and the following template to develop a class Bubble.java that can be called from the test program Sorter.java.

Testing Program Behavior

We know that as the array size increases, then the time for the sort should tend to increase proportionally since this is basically a CPU-intensive exercise. So part of our test will be to look for this trend.

Which algorithm is faster? The answer to this question should show up in your data. The testing is organized in the following table in terms of a performance analysis of the algorithms.

Some Performance Analysis.
After your program is ready, do the runs indicated in the following table, fill out the table with the millisecond values, and plot the results. Time permitting, do each run three times and plot these values.

Algorithm Type	Array Size		
	5000	10,000	15,000
Bubble			
Selection			

What do you notice?

_____

What is your interpretation of these results?

_____

Screen Shot of Program Behavior

The following is a screen shot of the Sorter.java program with the print statement suppressed. This run was for an array size of 1000. We can see that the Selection sort took 60 milliseconds whereas the Bubble Sort took 160 milliseconds. The time on your computer may be significantly different from this. Why? What will most likely be the same?

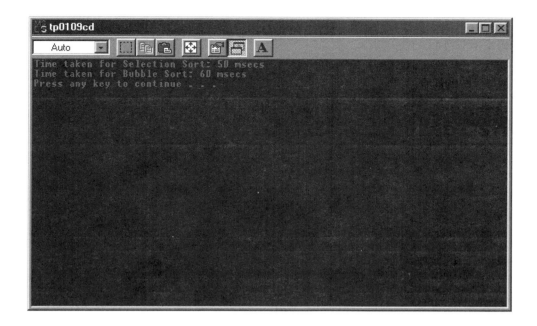

Download or obtain an electronic copy of the test program for this lab, Sorter.java. This is your program to test your work with.

Sorter.java creates an array for specified number of elements. It sorts the array with Selection Sort, and Bubble Sort calculates the time the sorting takes in each case and prints this time to the screen in time units of milliseconds. The following is the code.

```java
public class Sorter {

//
//
//
//

public static void main(String[] args) {

        int[] selectionSortArray, bubbleSortArray;

        selectionSortArray = new int[1000];
        bubbleSortArray = new int[1000];

        long start, end;

        for (int i = 0; i < selectionSortArray.length; i++){
                selectionSortArray[i] =    (int)((Math.random()
* 1000));
                bubbleSortArray[i] = selectionSortArray[i];
        }

        start = System.currentTimeMillis();
        SelectionSort.sort(selectionSortArray);
        end = System.currentTimeMillis();

        System.out.println("Time taken for Selection Sort: "
+ (end - start) + " msecs");

        start = System.currentTimeMillis();
        BubbleSort.sort(bubbleSortArray);
        end = System.currentTimeMillis();
```

```
            System.out.println("Time taken for Bubble Sort: " +
    (end - start) + " msecs");


        }


}
```

Download or obtain an electronic copy from your instructor of the program SelectionSort.java. This is the complete and will be exercised by the program Sorter.java.

```
public class SelectionSort
{
    /*****************************************************
     *Precondition:
     *Every indexed variable of the array a has a value.
     *Action: Sorts the array a so that
     *a[0] <= a[1] <= ... <= a[a.length - 1].
     *****************************************************/
    public static void sort(int[] a)
    {
        int index, indexOfNextSmallest;
        for (index = 0; index < a.length - 1; index++)
        {//Place the correct value in a[index]:
            indexOfNextSmallest = indexOfSmallest(index, a);
            interchange(index,indexOfNextSmallest, a);
            //a[0] <= a[1] <=...<= a[index] and these are
            the
            //smallest of the original array elements.
            //The remaining positions contain the rest of
            //the original array elements.
        }
    }


    /*********************************************************
     *Precondition: i and j are legal indexes for the array
a.
     *Postcondition:
     *The values of a[i] and a[j] have been interchanged.

    *********************************************************/
    private static void interchange(int i, int j, int[] a)
    {
        int temp;
        temp = a[i];
        a[i] = a[j];
        a[j] = temp;//original value of a[i]
    }


    /***************************************************
     *Returns the index of the smallest value among
     *a[startIndex], a[startIndex+1], ... a[a.length-1]
     ***************************************************/
    private static int indexOfSmallest(int startIndex, int[]
a)
    {
        int min = a[startIndex];
        int indexOfMin = startIndex;
        int index;
        for (index = startIndex + 1; index < a.length;
index++)
```

```
                if (a[index] < min)
                {
                    min = a[index];
                    indexOfMin = index;
                    //min is the smallest of a[startIndex]
through a[index]
                }

        return indexOfMin;
    }
}
```

Download or obtain an electronic copy from your instructor of the template below for
BubbleSort.java. This is the bulk of your programming work for this lab. Your job is
to complete this template so that it can be used in Sorter.java to fill in the preceding
table for the Performance Analysis exercise.

Sorter.java creates an array for specified number of elements. It sorts the array with
Selection Sort, and Bubble Sort calculates the time the sorting takes in each case and
prints this time to the screen in time units of milliseconds. The following is the code.

```
public class SelectionSort
{
    /**************************************************
     *Precondition:
     *Every indexed variable of the array a has a value.
     *Action: Sorts the array a so that
     *a[0] <= a[1] <= ... <= a[a.length - 1].
     **************************************************/
    public static void sort(int[] a)
    {
        int index, indexOfNextSmallest;
        for (index = 0; index < a.length - 1; index++)
        {//Place the correct value in a[index]:
            indexOfNextSmallest = indexOfSmallest(index, a);
            interchange(index,indexOfNextSmallest, a);
            //a[0] <= a[1] <=...<= a[index] and these are
            the
            //smallest of the original array elements.
            //The remaining positions contain the rest of
            //the original array elements.
        }
    }


    /*************************************************************
     *Precondition: i and j are legal indexes for the array
a.
     *Postcondition:
     *The values of a[i] and a[j] have been interchanged.

    *************************************************************/
    private static void interchange(int i, int j, int[] a)
    {
        int temp;
        temp = a[i];
        a[i] = a[j];
        a[j] = temp;//original value of a[i]
    }


    /**************************************************
     *Returns the index of the smallest value among
     *a[startIndex], a[startIndex+1], ... a[a.length-1]
```

```
                  *************************************************/
        private static int indexOfSmallest(int startIndex, int[]
a)
        {
            int min = a[startIndex];
            int indexOfMin = startIndex;
            int index;
            for (index = startIndex + 1; index < a.length;
index++)
                if (a[index] < min)
                {
                    min = a[index];
                    indexOfMin = index;
                    //min is the smallest of a[startIndex]
through a[index]
                }

            return indexOfMin;
        }
}
```

ANSWERS TO THE PRELAB PRACTICE QUIZ

1. array

2. selection, bubble

3. 0 5 10 15 20 25 30 35 40 45
   There is a space between each number, and the last thing printed out is a space at the end of the line.

4. ```
   int[ ] scores = { 97, 45, 100, 34, 42 };
   int N = (int) value;
   ```

5. 5 2 1 8 4
   2 1 5 4 8
   1 2 4 5 8

6. 5 2 1 8 4
   1 5 2 8 4
   1 2 5 8 4
   1 2 4 5 8
   ```

LABORATORY 7   Inheritance

OVERVIEW

In this laboratory exercise, you will complete an exercise to go over the basic concepts from Chapter 7, "Inheritance." You will be given a base class, and then you will create a derived class from the base class. The driver program to test the inheritance relationship is provided, but your instructor may want to add testing to this.

OBJECTIVES

Work with and develop Java programs to become familiar with and learn about

- Understanding a base or super class

- Developing a derived class from a base class
    - Using super( )
    - Overriding base class methods

- Testing the inheritance relationship using a driver program.

TEXT REFERENCE

This lab assumes that Chapter 7 has been covered in the lecture. The student should specifically review topics from Chapter 7 before attempting this Lab. These topics include those discussed in the Objectives.

PRELAB PRACTICE QUIZ

In each sentence , fill in the blanks with appropriate answers or supply a word that makes the sentence correct.

1. The expression super. outputInfo( ) in a method is a call to the outputInfo method in the _____.

2. You can redefine a method from a base class so that it has a different definition in the derived class. This is called _____ the method definition.

3. _____ methods of the base class are not inherited by the derived class.

4. If you are defining a class intended to be a derived class of some base class, then what important word must go in the declaration line of the new derived class? _____.

5. Go to the Programming Exercises section of this lab and read the description of the base class Employee and the derived class HourlyEmployee. In the space below, represent this inheritance relationship using a UML diagram using Display 7.6 page 426 of the text as a reference example.

PROGRAMMING EXERCISES

There are three related programming exercises. The first is to study a base class, the Employee that is complete. Next create a derived class, the HourlyEmployee, from this base class using the class shell given in part 2. In the third exercise, you will use a driver program to test these classes and the inheritance relationship.

1. The Base Class Employee

    Your instructions are to study this complete class, the Employee class, in preparation for developing an HourlyEmployee class as a derived class Employee.

    Program Requirements (complete)

```
/**
 * Employee.java
 *
 *
 *
 */


public class Employee
{
    //static variable unique for all objects in the class
    private static int CURRENT_ID = 1000;
  //private int CURRENT_ID = 1000;
    //Instance Variables
    private String name;
    private double yearsPay;

    //Special attribute that should only be set at creation.
    //You are given an id number when you are born (SSN) &
    you can't change it
    private int idNumber;

    //Constructors
    /**
       Construct a new employee (default constructor)
       Default values are "no name yet" and $0.00
    */
    public Employee()
    {
this("no name yet", 0.0);
    }

    /**
       Construct a new employee
       @param name The new employee's name.
    */
    public Employee(String name)
    {
this(name, 0.0);
    }

    public Employee(String name, double yearsPay)
    {
this.name = name;
this.yearsPay = yearsPay;

//assign this employee the current id number and increment it
    //so the next employee created gets the next number
        //this ensures the id numbers will be unique
        //Your TA will explain in detail
```

Laboratory 7 Inheritance   *59*

```java
            this.idNumber = CURRENT_ID++;
            System.out.println(CURRENT_ID);
        }

        //Accessor Methods
        /**
           Get the value of name.
           @return the value of name.
        */
        public String getName()
        {
            return name;
        }

        /**
         * Get the value of idNumber.
         * @return Value of idNumber.
         */
        public int getIdNumber()
        {
            return idNumber;
        }

        /**
         * Get the value of yearsPay.
         * @return Value of yearsPay.
         */
        public double getYearsPay()
        {
            return yearsPay;
        }

        //Mutators - notice you shouldn't set the id number
        /**
           Set the value of name.
           @param newName The valuCURRENT_IDe to assign to name.
        */
        public void setName(String newName)
        {
            name = newName;
        }

        /**
        super.outputInfo();      * Set the value of yearsPay.
         * @param v  Value to assign to yearsPay.
         */
        public void setYearsPay(double yearsPay)
        {
            this.yearsPay = yearsPay;
        }

        /**
           Output the employee info
        */
        public void outputInfo()
        {
            System.out.println("\nEmployee: \t" + getName());
            System.out.println("  id number: \t" +
        getIdNumber());
            System.out.println("  wages: \t" + getYearsPay());
        }
    }
```

2. The Derived Class HourlyEmployee

Use the following class template to complete the HourlyEmployee class. Specifically, you are to complete the method bodies so that this is a working program.

```
/**
 * HourlyEmployee.java
 *
 *
 *
 */

public class HourlyEmployee extends Employee
{
    //some static variables (same for all HourlyEmployee
    objects)
    private static final int INITIAL_HOURS = 0;
    private static final double MINIMUM_WAGE = 5.5;

    //Instance Variables

    /**
       Default constructor.
    */
    public HourlyEmployee()
    {

    }

    /**
       Constructor.
       @param name The employee's name
    */
    public HourlyEmployee(String name)
    {

    }

    /**
       Constructor.
       @param name The employee's name
       @param rate The hourly pay this employee receives
@param hours The number of hours worked by this employee.
    */
public HourlyEmployee(String name, double rate, int hours)
    {

    }

    //Accessor methods
    /**
     * Get the value of hourlyRate.
     * @return Value of hourlyRate.
     */
    public double getHourlyRate()
    {

    }

    /**
     * Get the value of hours.
     * @return Value of hours.
     */
      public int getHours()
      {
```

```
        }

        //Mutators
        /**
         * Set the value of hourlyRate.
         * @param rate  Value to assign to hourlyRate.
         */
        public void setHourlyRate(double rate)
        {

        }

        /**
         * Set the value of hours.
         * @param hours  Value to assign to hours.
         */
        public void setHours(int hours)
        {

        }

        /**
         * Set the value of yearsPay.
         * @param rate The hourly pay this employee receives
         * @param hours The number of hours worked by this
           employee.
         */
        public void setYearsPay(double rate, int hours)
        {

        }

        /**
            Output the pertinent HourlyEmployee info
        */
        public void outputInfo()
        {

        }

} // HourlyEmployee
```

3. The UseEmployee Class

Testing Program Behavior

Now test the HourlyEmployee class you developed in part 2 using the following complete program. Your instructor may want you to add test cases to this program.

```
/**
 * UseEmployee.java
 *
 *
 */

public class UseEmployee {

    public static void main(String[] args)
    {
    HourlyEmployee sue = new HourlyEmployee("Fred
        Clampitts", 7.50, 200);
    Employee jon = new Employee("John Difficultis",
        40000);
    HourlyEmployee Chester = new HourlyEmployee("Chester
        Wampitt", 7.50, 200);
    sue.outputInfo();
    jon.outputInfo();
    Chester.outputInfo();
    }

} // UseEmployee
```

Screen Shot of Program Behavior

The following is a screen shot of the program output for a particular set of data.

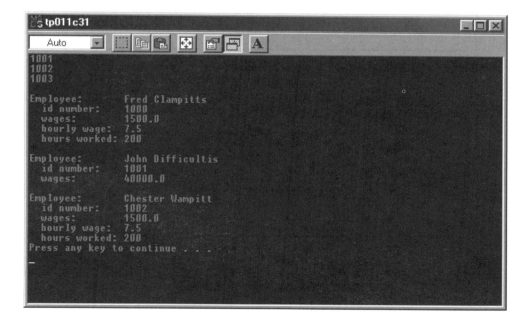

ANSWERS TO THE PRELAB PRACTICE QUIZ

1. base class

2. overriding

3. private

4. extends

5.

```
Employee

-CURRENT ID : int
-name : String
-yearspay : double

+ getName () : String
+ getIdNumber () : int
+ getYearsPay () : double
+ setName ( String newName ) : void
+ setYearsPay ( double yearsPay ); void
+ outputInfo () : void
```

```
HourlyEmployee

-INITIAL_HOURS : int
-MINIMUM_WAGE : double
-hourly_rate : double
-hours_worked : int

+ getHourlyRate () : double
+ getHours () : int
+ setHourlyRate ( double rate ) : void
+ setName ( String newName ) : void
+ setYearsPay ( double rate, int hours ); void
+ outputInfo () : void
```

OVERVIEW

In this laboratory exercise, you will work with the Exception class and learn how to incorporate this into your programming. Until now, we have made assumptions that a user will "do the right thing" when using our programs. So if a program asks for a length of the side of a triangle, then we have assumed that no one would enter –10! An exception is a way of handling an unexpected condition that the program may encounter in executing. These conditions can be simple, like the preceding one, or more complicated, such as a failed attempt to make a connect ion to a data source needed for your program such as an Oracle database. In this case, we would want to "throw" an SQLException. Probably we would not want to handle it at the database connection level but rather throw it up to the user interface level.

Hence, in introducing Exception programming we are recognizing that in a given block of code things may go as we expect or something unusual may happen. In the case of the latter situation we handle it in a separate block of code. This is all accomplished by dividing the usual block of code into "try" and "catch" blocks.

These exercises in the lab with Exceptions will also make use of your earlier study of classes and inheritance. Inheritance will enter into consideration when you define Exceptions and extend the Exception class.

Key to success in this lab is proper use of the instance variable "message" and the method "getMessage" of the Exception class and in the case of user defined Exceptions the use of "super()".

OBJECTIVES

The objectives of this laboratory are

To learn and implement exception handling in Java
To understand the use of the keywords 'try', 'catch', 'throws', and 'throw'
To learn how to use Javadoc to produce program documentation

TEXT REFERENCE

This lab assumes that Chapter 8 has been covered in the lecture. In this lab you will use the Java base class Exception, which has common predefined exceptions such as

IOException
ClassNotFoundException
FileNotFoundException

You will apply material learned in Chapter 7 to write an Exception class of your own to use in this lab. Since we will also run the Javadoc program to produce documentation, you should read Appendix 9.

PRELAB PRACTICE QUIZ

1. Exactly what output will be produced when the following class is compiled and run?

```
public class Testing {

    public static void main(String[ ] args)
    {
        String name = "John";
        int age = 156;
    try
    {
        if(name==null)
            throw new Exception("Where is the name?");
        else System.out.println("Hello " + name);
        if(age>120)
            throw new AgeException("Oh, come on, you can not
            be that old");
        else
            System.out.println("you are " + age + "years
old");
        }
        catch(AgeException ae)
        {
            System.out.println("From user defined
            exception");
            System.out.println(ae.getMessage());
        }

        catch(Exception e)
        {
            System.out.println("You have made some error");
            System.out.println(e.getMessage());

        }

    String junk = SavitchIn.readLine();
    }
}

 class AgeException extends Exception
{
    public AgeException()
    {
        super("age exception");
    }
    public AgeException(String message)
    {
        super(message);
    }
}
```

2. In the preceding code, find and write out the catch block that is executed.

3. Is the following statement legal:\?

```
Exception myException = new Exception("Hi there");
```

PROGRAMMING EXERCISES

You need to obtain a copy of the following files or download them from your lab or course Web site:

1. Person.java
2. UsePerson.java
3. InvalidHeightException.java

InvalidHeightexception.java is complete. No modification needs to be made to this file. Here is your part:

1. Modify Person.java by adding exception handling techniques to use InvalidHeightException.java where appropriate.

2. Create InvalidYearException.java to catch the exception of when the current year is less than the person's birth year. You need to extend Exception in creating this class. (It should be similar to InvalidHeightException.java.)

3. Modify UsePerson.java to take advantage of both exception handling classes.

4. Note that the programs are given in the format described in Appendix 9, "Javadoc." Read over this material and then at the DOS prompt run

    javadoc Person.java

    This will give you an idea of how Sun documents programs and program requirements.

The following are copies of these programs and files that are provided to you in this lab.

Person.java

```
/**
 * Person.java
 * Description:  This lab is an exercise in exception handling,
 *               emphasis on keywords try, catch, throw, throws.
 *
 * Note the use of javadoc comments
 *
 */

public class Person {

    // Instance variables
    private String name;
    private int yearBorn;
    private double height;

    // Constructors -- Set default values if none given

    /**
        Default Constructor.
    */
    public Person() {
       this("no name yet", 1900, 6.0);
    }

    /**
```

```java
        Constructor.
        @param name The person's name.
    */
    public Person(String name) {
        this(name, 1900, 6.0);
    }

    /**
        Constructor.
        @param yearBorn The person's year of birth.
    */
    public Person(int yearBorn) {
        this("no name yet", yearBorn, 6.0);
    }

    /**
        Constructor.
        @param height The person's height in feet.
    */
    public Person(double height) {
        this("no name yet", 1900, height);
    }

    /**
        Constructor.
        @param name The person's name.
        @param yearBorn The person's year of birth.
        @param height The person's height in feet.
    */
    public Person(String name, int yearBorn, double height) {
        this.name = name;
        this.yearBorn = yearBorn;
        this.height = height;
    }

    // Overloading the set accessor method

    /**
        Set the value of name.
        @param name The person's name.
    */
    public void set(String name) {
        this.name = name;
    }

    /**
        Set the value of yearBorn.
        @param yearBorn The person's year of birth.
    */
    public void set(int yearBorn) {
        this.yearBorn = yearBorn;
    }

    /**
        Set the value of height.
        @param height The person's height in feet.
    */
    public void set(double height) {
        this.height = height;
    }

    /**
        Set the person's name, yearBorn, and height.
        @param name The person's name.
        @param yearBorn The person's year of birth.
        @param height The person's height in feet.
    */
    public void set(String name, int yearBorn, double height) {
```

```
            set(name);
            set(yearBorn);
            set(height);
        }

        /**
           Calculate the person's age based on the current year.
           @param year The current year.
        */
        private int calcAge(int year) {
            return year - yearBorn;
        }

        /**
           Displays the person's age in years.
        */
        public void getAge() {
            System.out.print("What is the current year? ");
            int currentYear = SavitchIn.readLineInt();
            System.out.println(name + " is " + calcAge(currentYear) + "
            years old.");
        }

        /**
           Displays all of the person's information.
        */
        public void displayInfo() {
            System.out.println("\n\nThe person's name is " + name +
".");
            System.out.println(name + " was born in " + yearBorn + ".");
            System.out.println(name + " is " + height + " feet tall.");
        }

} // Person
```

InvalidHeightException.java

```
/**
 * InvalidHeightException.java
 *
 *
 *
 *
 * @author
 * @version
 */

public class InvalidHeightException extends Exception {

    public InvalidHeightException(double height) {

        super("<* InvalidHeightException Generated for height = "
        + height + " *>");
    }

} // InvalidHeightException
```

UsePerson.java

```java
/**
 * UsePerson.java
 *
 *
 *
 *
 */

public class UsePerson {

    public UsePerson() {

    }

    public static void main(String[] args) {

        //Create a new person p1
        Person p1 = new Person("John", 1972, -5.5);
        p1.displayInfo();
        p1.getAge();

        //Change the values in p2
        Person p2 = new Person();
        p2.set("John Johnson");
        p2.set(-6.1);
        p2.displayInfo();
        p2.getAge();

        //Change the values again
        Person p3 = new Person();
        p3.set("John Johnson III", 2030, 6.3);
        p3.displayInfo();
        p3.getAge();
    }

} // UsePerson
```

Testing Program Behavior

Now test the class you developed using the program UsePerson.java. You may want to add additional test cases.

Screen Shot of Program Behavior

The following is a screen shot of the program output for a particular set of data.

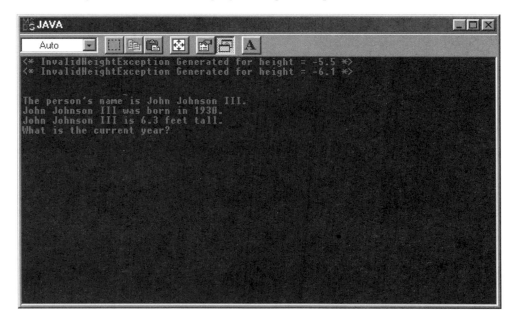

ANSWERS TO THE PRELAB PRACTICE QUIZ

1. ANSWER:
    Hello John
    From user defined exception
    Oh, come on, you can not be that old

2.
```
catch(AgeException ae)
{
System.out.println("From user defined exception");
System.out.println(ae.getMessage());
}
```

3. Yes

OVERVIEW

In this laboratory exercise, you will write a program TextFileIO.java. This program will

Read a line from the console using BufferedReader class.
Write that line to a file using PrintWriter class.
Read a line back from to verify the write.

You will gain experience in creating files, connecting to output streams for writing, closing files, and opening files for reading using input streams.

OBJECTIVES

Work with and develop Java programs to become familiar with and learn about Text file input and output. In particular, you will gain experience in

Opening and closing input and output streams
Using the BufferedReader class to take a file name as an argument, producing an input stream of the class BufferedReader, and connecting your program to the named file so that your program can receive input from the file
Using the PrintWriter class to take a file name as an argument, producing an output stream of the class PrintWriter, and connecting your program to the named file so that your program can sent output to the file
Closing input and output streams and the importance of doing this
Writing try and catch blocks in this new programming setting of text file I/O

If you would like to reference the Java documentation, then browse http://java.sun.com/j2se/1.4.2/docs/api/. Select the java.io class and then look for the subclasses InputStream and OutputStream. From this you will see that we have made a start but have barely scratched the surface in java.io!

TEXT REFERENCE

This lab assumes that the first part of Chapter 10, "Streams and File I/O," has been covered in the lecture on text file I/O. You should also review the basic steps in creating try and catch blocks from Chapter 8, "Exceptions."

PRELAB PRACTICE QUIZ

In each sentence, fill in the blanks with appropriate answers or supply a word that makes the sentence correct.

1. To open an input stream using the file "numbers.txt", the following code is executed:

    ```
    BufferedReader inputStream = new BufferedReader( new
    Filereader("numbers.txt"));
    ```

    Write a line of code that will close this file.

    _____

2. What statement do you need to include in your program file to tell the Java compiler and linker that your program will need the file I/O classes discussed in Chapter 9?

    _____

3. The following is a fragment of code from a program. In the blanks explain what this program is doing.

    ```
    public textFileParse(String filename)
            {

            try
            {
                    BufferedReader inText= new BufferedReader(new
                    FileReader(filename));

                    //create the PatientDetail object
                    PatientDetail ptDetail = new PatientDetail();

                    String lineInFile = inText.readLine();

                    while(lineInFile!=null)
                    {
                    if(lineInFile.startsWith("RunNumber"))
                    {
                    handleRunNumber(lineInFile,ptDetail);
                    }

                    if(lineInFile.startsWith("SubjectNumber"))
                            {
                    handleSubjectNumber(lineInFile,ptDetail);
                    }
                    if(lineInFile.startsWith("SubjectName"))
                    {
                    handleSubjectName(lineInFile,ptDetail);
                    }

                    lineInFile = inText.readLine();
                    }

            /*just for printing*/
            System.out.println(ptDetail);

            inText.close();
            }
            catch(IOException ie)
            {
    ```

```
                System.out.println("Error in Reading Text
                File"+ie.getMessage());
        }
```

_____

_____

PROGRAMMING EXERCISES

In this lab, you will

1. Use the BufferedReader Stream Class to read input from the console or keyboard by connecting an input stream to the keyboard. You will need to use a statement like this:

```
BufferedReader inputstream
= new BufferedReader(new InputStreamReader(System.in));
```

System.in refers to the so-called standard input stream for the program, which is set normally set to the console.

2. This programming assignment only requires you to read in one line of text from the keyboard. You can enter more by using a while or other loop statement. This data will be stored in a String variable.

3. This line of text should be written out to the text file using the PrintWriter Stream class. This will involve creating the file, opening it, and connecting it to your program output stream PrintWriter object.

4. Finally, use the BufferedReader Stream Class to create another input stream to read from the file you just created. Verify the write was made and that the file contains the line of text that you typed in.

5. Use try blocks with appropriate catch blocks for the creation of the input and output streams in Steps 3 and 4. Use one try block with catch blocks for each separate operation. Remember to close all input and output streams at the appropriate points in the program.

6. In Part 4, do a second read from the file that you created and wrote a line of text. What happens? _____

7. What happens if for example you do not close the PrintWriter output stream in Step 3 after writing to the file and then you try to read from this file? _____

Screen Shot of Program Behavior

The following is a screen shot of the program output for a particular set of data.

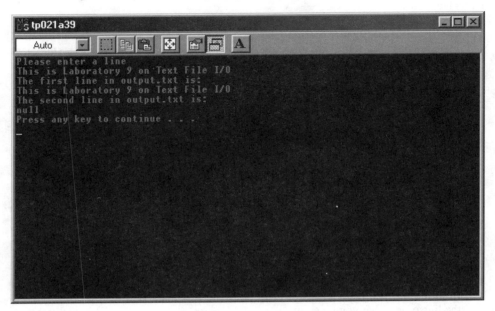

ANSWERS TO THE PRELAB PRACTICE QUIZ

1. inputStream.close( );

2. import java.io.*;

3. This is an example where a file is being scanned for certain information. In this case, the program is part of processing medical test data and a file is being scanned for specific information to store in a Patient Record. The method readLine of the BufferedReader object inText reads in a line at a time of the file. The line is checked for keywords: RunNumber, SubjectNumber, and SubjectName. For each of these words that the line contains, the line is processed further by a method that essentially extracts information and stores this information.

Answers to the questions in the Programming Exercises

You get a null.
Same thing.

OVERVIEW

In this laboratory exercise, you will get experience reading and writing to binary files. You will also write to a text file the same thing that you write to the binary file.

This lab is about storing data in files. We stored data using arrays and vectors but there is a big difference here. This storage is permanent or as long as we want it to be; whereas, in the other methods, the storage only lasts as long as the program is running. When you write data to a file, it is permanent in the sense that the data are stored on a hard drive or other medium and the file is there until it is deleted by you or someone else who has that permission on the file (assuming no catastrophic events and a good backup or fault-tolerant system!).

In Laboratory 6, we investigated the performance of two sort algorithms and also indicated other factors that can influence this type of CPU-bound task, such as processor speed. Processor speed is important in scientific research and calculation. However, it is usually not the critical factor or bottleneck in business applications. In business, the most important task is usually processing many millions transactions such as occur in day-to-day life. Examples are grocery stores, airline reservations, course registrations, hotel reservations, and purchases at stores everywhere. All of these involve keeping permanent records of what happened, and this is File I/O. For this reason, computer hardware and software designers work closely with customers with businesses like these and gain a good understanding of what the customer's expectation is in terms of tps (transactions per second). Special tests or benchmarks are designed to simulate the customer's business under heavy File I/O loads. Often the customer expects a proof of concept demonstration early in the presale process with a demonstration at delivery time of the required tps using the customer's application software.

OBJECTIVES

The main objectives of this lab are

- To learn to read input from different file types
- To learn to write output to different file types
- To understand the proper use of exception handling with files
- To use and understand the File object

In general, the objective is to gain additional experience using this method of storing data in files instead of arrays, vectors, variables, or class definitions. You will create files and then use methods to manipulate the files objects by reading, writing, and using other files methods.

TEXT REFERENCE

This lab assumes that the latter part of Chapter 9 has been covered in the lecture—in particular, the section on the File object and reading and writing to binary files.

Specific items to go over before the lab are

- Using the class Printwriter to write to a text file and BufferedReader to read from a text file
- The class File and its methods such as exists( ), canRead ( ), canWrite( )
- Using the class ObjectOutputStream to write to a text file and ObjectInputStream to read from a text file and their methods to write and read one byte at a time
- File I/O Exceptions
- The special case for writing strings and using the method writeUTF( ) of the ObjectOutputStream class

PRELAB PRACTICE QUIZ

Answer the following questions in the space provided.

1. Write a line of code to create an output stream of type ObjectOutputStream that is named outFile and is connected to a binary file named file1.dat.

_____

2. Write a line of code to create an input stream of type ObjectInputStream that is named inFile and is connected to a binary file named file1.dat.

_____

3. Write a line of code that will close the stream inFile created in question 2.

_____

4. Analyze the following program and write a brief description of what it does.

_____

```java
import java.io.*;

public class FileWriter1 {

    public FileWriter1() {

    }


    public static void main(String[] args) {
        System.out.print("Enter the name of the desired output file: ");
        String fileName = SavitchIn.readLine();

        try
            {

                ObjectOutputStream outputStream = new
                ObjectOutputStream (new FileOutputStream (fileName));

                int numItems, userInt;
                char userInputChar, userChar;
                double userDouble;
                boolean userBoolean;
                String userString;

                System.out.println("How many data items will you be
                entering? ");
                numItems = SavitchIn.readLineInt();

                outputStream.writeInt(numItems);

                for(int i = 1; i <= numItems; i++)
                    {
                        System.out.print("\nWhat is the type for item
                        #" + i + " (i,c,b, d,s)? ");
                        userInputChar =
                        SavitchIn.readLineNonwhiteChar();
                        outputStream.writeChar(userInputChar);
```

```java
                    switch (userInputChar)
                        {
                            case 'b':
                            case 'B':
                            {
                            System.out.print("Enter a boolean:
                            false/true ");
                            userBoolean =
                            SavitchIn.readLineBoolean();

                            outputStream.writeBoolean(userBoolean);
                            }
                            break;

                        case 'i':
                        case 'I':
                            {
                            System.out.print("Enter an integer:
                            ");
                            userInt = SavitchIn.readLineInt();
                            outputStream.writeInt(userInt);
                            }
                            break;
                        case 'c':
                        case 'C':
                            {
                            System.out.print("Enter a char: ");
                            userChar =

                            SavitchIn.readLineNonwhiteChar();
                            outputStream.writeChar(userChar);
                            }
                            break;
                        case 'd':
                        case 'D':
                            {
                            System.out.print("Enter a double:
                            ");
                            userDouble =
                            SavitchIn.readLineDouble();

                            outputStream.writeDouble(userDouble);
                            }
                            break;
                        case 's':
                        case 'S':
                            {
                                System.out.print("Enter a String:
                                    ");
                                String useString;
                                userString = SavitchIn.readLine();
                                outputStream.writeUTF(userString);
                            }
                            break;
                        default:
                            {
                                //This case doesn't really need to
                                  be handled
                                //based on the problem
                                specification!
                                System.out.println("\nUnknown
                                Input");
                            }
                        }
                    }
System.out.println("\n\n<* The file " + fileName + "  has been
created with your data! *>");
                outputStream.close();
```

```
        }
    catch (IOException e)
        {
            System.out.println("\n\n<* Error Opening " + fileName
+ " *>");
System.out.println("<* The Following IOException Was Generated: "
+ e.getMessage());
        }
    }
} // FileWriter
```

PROGRAMMING EXERCISES

You should download or obtain from your lab instructor the file, bin_read.dat. You are to create a Java program named FileReader.java that will read the file bin_read.dat and do the following:

- Read the binary file whose format is an integer giving the number of entries and then an integer, a double, a character, a Boolean, and a string. Each value is preceeded by a code of its type (i,c,b, d,s).
- Output the file to the screen.
- Write this data to a binary file and to a text file.
- Use the File object to display
  - Whether or not the file exists
  - The file size in bytes
  - The path of the file
- Make the program more general so that it will read any binary file with an integer giving the number of entries first and then entries having the data types mentioned previously.

Testing Program Behavior

Now test the program you developed by using the program in the prelab quiz.

Screen Shot of Program Behavior.

The following is a screen shot of the program output.

ANSWERS TO THE PRELAB PRACTICE QUIZ

1. ObjectOutputStream outFile = new
   ObjectOutputStream("file1.dat");

2. ObjectIntputStream inFile = new
   ObjectInputStream("file1.dat");

3. inFile.close( );

4. The program is doing something similar to what is in the preceding screen display.
   The user specifies the file name and then data are written to and read from the file.
   Some methods are tested.

LABORATORY 11   Dynamic Data Structures—VECTORS

OVERVIEW

In this laboratory exercise, you will become familiar with using vectors. Vectors can be thought of as arrays that can grow and shrink in size while your program is running. Vectors are one of two types of data structures discussed in Chapter 10 that can grow and shrink in size while your program is executing. The other is linked list data structures. Linked list data structures will be the subject of the next laboratory. Because of this common feature, these data structures are referred to as dynamic data structures.

You will be able to contrast the differences, advantages, and disadvantages of vectors as compared to arrays. Arrays are generally easier to use and perform better with respect to execution time in large data situations. On the other hand, vectors expand more or less "automatically" as needed by the program or you can specify at the time of the creation of the vector object the unit in which the vector will increment its size. Like arrays, vectors can store objects and the objects do not need to be of the same type. That is, a vector can store Integer class objects (but not ints or primitive types) and that same vector can also store Species objects and other object types. Arrays cannot store different kinds of objects. When you remove an object from a vector, this means that you must cast the object to its intended type.

In this lab, you will need to define and utilize a vector that stores "items". We will suppose that we are programming something that could be used to store items on an Internet or eBusiness shopping cart. You will need to define a class called "item". Item will contain information about a particular product such as a book, its cost, and the quantity you purchase. You can purchase any number of items and when done you must have your bill totaled. This should be an interesting lab!

OBJECTIVES

This lab provides opportunity to gain some experience using vectors and classes in a practical setting. Specifically, you will

- Define and use a class for storing information about particular items purchased.
- Use a vector to store the items.
- Use a main program to test the vector method of storing items for purchase and total up the bill.

TEXT REFERENCE

This lab assumes that Section 1 of Chapter 10 has been covered in the lecture. You should also review the section in Chapter 5 on "Wrapper Classes." Review class definitions and methods from Chapters 4 and 5. Review vector methods, such as how to add elements to a vector and access them. Study examples in the text about casting objects to their types when they are removed or copied from vector storage.

Part of the lab involves a method that will total up the prices of all the items purchased. An output such as $1004.89887 does not look very business-like. Read Appendix 6, "The Decimal Format Class." You will use information in this appendix to format your bill so that it has the appearance of a bill total that you would present to a customer.

PRELAB PRACTICE QUIZ

In each sentence, fill in the blanks with appropriate answers or supply a word that makes the sentence correct.

1. Write one line of code to connect an integer value *n* to an object of type Integer denoted by *N*.

    _____

2. Write a line of code that will get the value stored in the Integer wrapper class object name *N* and store it in an integer variable named *k*.

    _____

3. _____ can be thought of as arrays that can shrink and grow in length.

4. The base type of all vectors is _____. Thus elements of a vector may be of any class type, but they cannot be of _____ type.

5. The definition of the class vector is in the package _____; hence any code that uses the vector class must contain the following normally at the start of the file:

    _____

6. Write the code necessary to create a vector *v* with initial capacity = 5.

    _____

PROGRAMMING EXERCISES

We want to design a program for a business situation such as an internet shopping basket where items are selected and put into a shopping basket. After the shopping is completed, the quantities of each item are used to compute the total bill for the order. Here are the steps to follow in developing this program.

1.   Create a class called Item. Item has these instance variables with access modifiers and types:

   - public String name;
   - public int quantity
   - public double unit_price

   Item has these methods:

   - public void print( ) to print out the values stored in the data above
   - public double extendedPrice(), a method that returns unit_price*quantity or the total dollar value of a quantity of particular items

   Include an appropriate constructor.

2.   Create a class called Order that is a derived class of Vector. Order does not need any instance variables. Order has these methods:

   - public void add(Item u), which adds Item objects to the vector element of this object.
   - public double totalPrice(). This is a method that computes the value of the order in dollars based on the items on the vector. It utilizes methods of the item class to compute the total value or contribution to the bill of each individual Item object.

3.   Create a test or driver program to test the classes developed previously.

Testing Program Behavior

Your test program should allow the user to input a number of items each with a quantity and total the bill. Your program should print out the detail of each item purchased and then under this print the total bill amount of the order in dollars. The bill amount should be in a common format such as $000,000.00. Read Appendix 6, "Decimal Format Class," to see how to do this.

Screen Shot of Program Behavior

The following is a screen shot of the program output for a particular set of input data. Here we assume we are at an Internet bookstore.

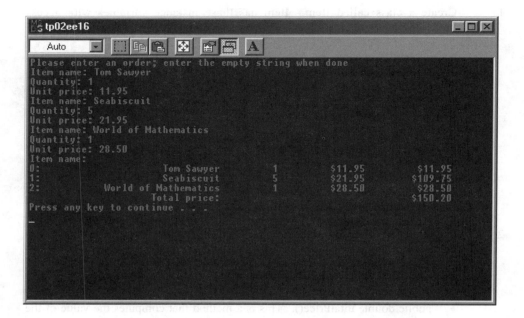

ANSWERS TO THE PRELAB PRACTICE QUIZ

1. Integer N = new Integer(n);

2. int k = N.intvalue( );

3. vectors

4. object, primitive

5. java.util

6. Vector v = new Vector(5);

Dynamic Data Structures— LINKED LISTS

OVERVIEW

In this laboratory exercise, you will work with linked lists. Linked lists are used to store data in a program. Arrays and vectors also do this. Each method has certain advantages and disadvantages. One big advantage of linked lists is that they are just enough just in time, so to speak. Memory space for arrays is allocated in contiguous segments, whereas memory for a linked list is allocated one node at a time as needed for a data item and the memory is not contiguous. This laboratory provides experience in programming with linked lists.

OBJECTIVES

Write Java programs to become familiar with and learn about

> Constructing list nodes and linked lists used to store
> Primitive data types
> Class data types
> Adding nodes to a linked list
> Deleting nodes from a linked list
> Computing the length of a linked list
> Working with other methods of a linked list

TEXT REFERENCE

This lab assumes that Chapter 10 been covered in the lecture. The student should specifically review topics from Chapter 10, Section 2, on linked lists before attempting this lab. These topics include the following:

> Linked data structures
> Inner classes and node inner classes
> Iterators

PRELAB PRACTICE QUIZ

In each sentence, fill in the blanks with appropriate answers or supply a word that makes the sentence correct.

1. Using a(n) _____ class makes StringLinkedList SelfContainted because it does not depend on a separate file.

2. An object that allows a program to step through a collection of objects and do some action on each one is called a(n) _____.

3. StringLinkedListSelfContained has an instance variable called _____ that is used to keep track of whrere the iteration is.

4. Suppose cursor refers to a node in a linked list. Which of the following Boolean expressions will be true when cursor refers to the tail node or last node of the list?

    a. cursor == null   b. cursor.data == null   c. cursor.link == null

    d. cursor.data == 0   e. None of these

5. Write a single statement that will create a small linked list with head reference and just one node. The node part contains the String "John". Do this so that the result will be as depicted in the following picture.

head

   _____

6. What changes are necessary to the file StringLinkedListSelfContained. java to convert it into a class with the exact same characteristics and methods but with the data type stored in the linked list changed to int?

   _____

7. Suppose that "head" is a reference to a linked list that this 400 nodes. Write a line of code that will delete all 400 values from the program.

   _____

PROGRAMMING EXERCISES

1. IntLinkedList

    Access your Text CD and go to the directory that has the Chapter 10 Source Code. Make the necessary changes StringLinkedListWithIterator.java so that it stores integer data instead of String data and convert the methods so that they handle integer data. Call your new class file IntLinkedListWithIterator.java.

    Write these methods and add them to the class file:

    ```
    public int tallyIt(int lower)
    {
    /** accepts an integer "lower" as a parameter and returns the
    number of data items on the list that are greater than "lower"
    **/
    }

    public void deleteFromList( int target)

    {
    /**
        Deletes all occurences of the target value from the list.
    Makes use of the internal iterator contained in the class
    IntLinkedListWithIterator.java.

        **/
    }
    ```

    Write a Test Program called IntLinkedListWithIteratorDemo.java that does the following:

    Creates an IntLinkedListWithIterator object called "list".
    Populates the list with N random integers between 1 and 100 where N is a positive integer specified by the user.
    Uses the method showList( ) to display "list".
    Uses the method tallyIt( ). For instance, tallyIt(50) should return something close to $N/2$ for N large. This can be used as an indicator of proper randomization.
    Removes all ListNodes on the LinkedList have data equal to "value", where "value" is a positive integer specified by the user.

Screen Shot of Program Behavior

The following is a sample of how the program should respond to various inputs. Your job is to write a program that does this.

```
tp0ac25e                                                          _ □ ✕
 Auto        ▼   ▦ ▤ ▤ | ▦ | ▦ ▦ | A
Enter the number of integers you want on the list.
4
4
List has 4 entries.
69
25
22
87
Enter your lower bound
50
The number of integers on the list
greater than 50 is 2
Do you want to remove a value from the list?
Enter Y for yes or N for No
Y
Enter the integer value that you want to delete all occurences from the list
22
All instances of 22 have been deleted.
Here is the new list
69
25
87
Now the length of the list is 3.
Press any key to continue . . .
```

Testing Program Behavior.

Test your program for faulty behavior.

Try generating small lists of 1, 2–10 nodes that you can see on the screen. Generate larger lists with 100 – 10,000 nodes. Use the tallyIt( ) method to test randomization and size. For instance, if you generate 10,000 nodes and enter 3,000 for a lower bound in the tallyIt( ) method, then you would expect to see a number something like 7,000 returned.

2. SpeciesLinkedListSelfContained

Implement SpeciesLinkedList, a Linked List for storing Species class Objects using StringLinkedListSelfContained class as reference. Access your Text CD and go to the directory that has the Chapter 10 Source Code and Species class code. Make the necessary changes to StringLinkedListSelfContained or use it as a reference to create a SpeciesLinkedList class using the following shell class. Follow the comments in the shell and write the code to complete the SpeciesLinkedList class.

```java
public class SpeciesLinkedList
{
   private SpeciesNode head;

    public SpeciesLinkedList()
    {
        head = null;
    }

    /*****************************************
     *Returns the number of nodes in the list.
     *****************************************/
  /**
   * @return - returns the number of nodes in the list
   */
   public int length()
```

```
        {
            //code to be supplied
        }


/***********************************************************************
 *Adds a node at the start of the list. The added node has addData
 *as its data. The added node will be the first node in the list.

 ***********************************************************************/
        /**
         * adds a node to the list
         * @param addData - Species Object to be added to the list
         */
        public void addANodeToStart(Species addData)
        {
            //code to be supplied
        }

        /**
         * deletes a node
         */
        public void deleteHeadNode()
        {
            //code to be supplied
        }

        /**
         * checks if a Species Object with the given speciesName
         exists in the list
         * @param speciesName - name of the Species name
         * @return - returns true if there is a SpeciesObject with
         the given Species name, else returns false
         *
         */
        public boolean onList(String speciesName)
        {

        }


/***********************************************************************
***
        *Finds the first node (SpeciesNode) containing the Species
         Object with the given name ,
        * and returns a reference to that node. If key is not in the
         list, null is returned.

***********************************************************************
**/
        private SpeciesNode Find(String speciesName)
        {
            //code to be supplied
        }

        /**
         * display all the nodes in the list
         */
        public void showList()
        {
            //code to be supplied
        }

        private class SpeciesNode
        {
            private Species speciesData;
            private SpeciesNode link;
```

```java
        public SpeciesNode()
        {
            link = null;
            speciesData = null;
        }

        public SpeciesNode(Species speciesData, SpeciesNode
linkValue)
            {
                this.speciesData = speciesData;
                link = linkValue;
            }
    }

    /**
     * create a linked list
     * create three Species Objects
     * add them to the list
     * display the list
     * prompt the user to enter a species name
     * find if the user entered species name is among the list
     * if a species name is found
     *      - display "Species species_name is one of the
number_of_species_in_list Species on the list"
     * else
     * - display "Species species_name is not one among the
number_of_species_in_list Species on the list"
     */
    public static void main(String args[])
    {
            SpeciesLinkedList list = new SpeciesLinkedList();

            //create three nodes and add them to the list
            //code to be supplied

            //display the list
            //code to be supplied

            //prompt the user for a species name to search in the
list
            //display the appropriate message
            //code to be supplied
    }
}
```

Screen Shot of Program Behavior

The following is a sample of how the program should respond to various inputs. Your job is to write a program that does this.

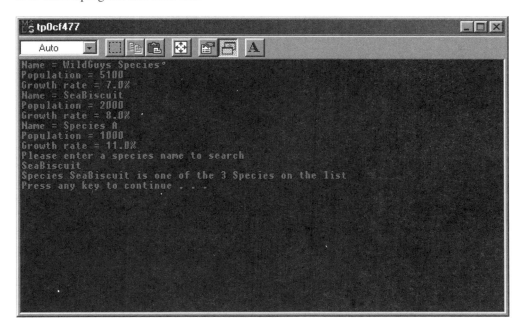

ANSWERS TO THE PRELAB PRACTICE QUIZ

1. inner

2. iterator

3. cursor

4. C

5. `ListNode head = new ListNode("John", null);`

6. In TextPad do a "Replace All" replacing every occurrence of "String" with "Int". Replace "Int" with "int" wherever the data type "int" is involved (used to be "String"). At line 68, replace with String "equals" method with "==" and be sure to balance parentheses. Rename the file IntLinkedListSelfContained.java and the constructor.

7. head = null;

OVERVIEW

In this laboratory exercise, you will develop a graphical user interface (GUI) using Swing. So far all the laboratories have used the simplest form of input and output. The user enters simple text at the keyboard, and simple text is sent to the screen as output. With the advent of MS Windows in the late 1980s and early 1990s, users began to expect that running programs should be as easy as possible with features such as menus and buttons. They no longer wanted "ugly" text-based screens; everything should be accessible through an icon on their desktop just as word processing, e-mail, and other office functions had become for them.

Today software development begins at the user or customer by understanding their requirements for good usability. If you are going to major in computer science, then one of your courses will probably be called software engineering or something like that. This subject deals with the process of developing high-quality software. Part of what is meant by "quality" is that the software satisfies the customer's requirements for usability.

Generally, customer requirements fall into two types: functional requirements and nonfunctional requirements. Functional requirements are what we usually think of. They are about what the software should do or provide to the user. Nonfunctional requirements or emergent properties of the software are overall properties or constraints that the software must have or satisfy. These include performance constraints such as a certain number of transactions per second (throughput) or response time, reliability or trouble-free operation, availability or uptime, and ease of use or usability.

In Laboratory 13, you will make using and testing a Linked List user friendly. We will put a GUI fron end on the Linked List of integers and make the Linked List methods easier to use.

OBJECTIVES

The objectives of this laboratory are

- To learn and implement basic features of GUI
- To understand the use of textfields
- To learn how to use buttons and action listeners

TEXT REFERENCE

This lab assumes that Chapter 13 has been covered in the lecture. In this lab, you will use objects such as

JFrames
JPanels, ContentPanes
JTextFields, Jbuttons, and JTextAreas
Action events, ActionListeners, and ActionPerformed methods

to put a user friendly front end on the IntLinkedList class. You will attach the methods of the IntLinkedList to buttons and the methods will be performed using ActionListeners for the buttons. Each method will be executed as a button is clicked on, an action event is generated, and the event is performed by an ActionPerformed associated with the ActionListener attached to the button. Data to be used in the methods will be entered into JTextFields and results or updates displayed in a JTextArea.

PRELAB PRACTICE QUIZ

In each sentence, fill in the blanks with appropriate answers or supply a word that makes the sentence correct.

1. The class _____ is the Swing class that you use to form a windowing GUI.

2. You can use a(n) _____ to add a string of text to a GUI.

3. The components in a container are arranged by an an object called a(n) _____.

4. A(n) _____ is a container object that is used to group components inside a larger container.

5. _____ and _____ are used for text input and output in a GUI constructed with Swing.

6. Suppose w is an object of the class JFrame. Give a Java statement that will declare a variable named contentPane and set it so that it names the content pane of w.

    _____

7. What import statement do you need to be able to use the type container? _____.

8. How does BorderLayout manager arrange components in a container?

9. Write an expression to convert the string "3.14159" to a double value 3.14159. Include it in an assignment statement that stores that value in the variable x of type double.

    _____

PROGRAMMING EXERCISES

Given the IntLinkedList class you worked with in Laboratory 11, develop the GUI for Linked List methods. Your GUI should support the following operations:

1. **Add a number to list.** GUI should allow the user to enter a number into a TextField and press the "add" button. Once the button is pressed, the number entered should be added to the list and an appropriate message should be displayed to the user into the TextArea.

2. **Delete the head from the list.** GUI should allow the user to delete the head node from the list by pressing a "delete" button. Once the button is pressed, the head node should be deleted from the list and an appropriate message should be displayed to the user into the TextArea.

3. **Display the list.** GUI should display the entire list by pressing a "display" button. Once the button is pressed, numbers in the list should be displayed to the user into the TextArea.

4. **Length of the List.** GUI should display the length of the list by pressing a "length" button. Once the button is pressed, the length of the list should be displayed to the user into the TextArea.

5. **Find a number on List.** GUI should allow the user to enter a number into a TextField and press the "find" button. Once the button is pressed, list should be checked for that number. Display an appropriate message to the user into the TextArea depending on whether the number is found or not found on the list.

The following is a sample of how the program should respond to various inputs. Your job is to write a program that does this.

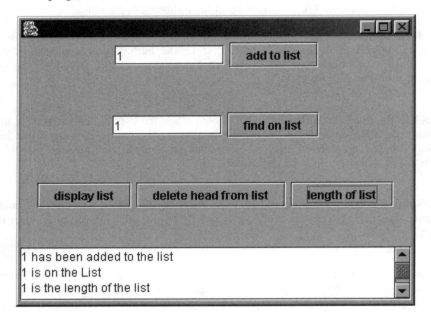

In this display, the text area at the bottom of the screen shows the events and their time order.

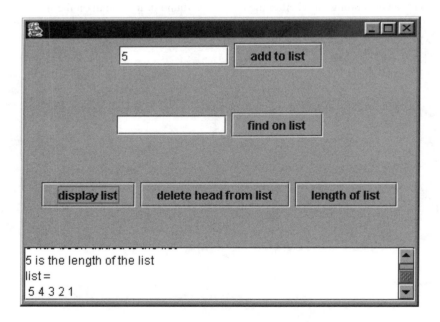

This view shows the GUI after 1, 2, 3, 4, 5 have been added to the list, the "length" button clicked, and then the "display list" button clicked.

Testing Program Behavior

Test your program for faulty behavior.

Minimally, you should test several cases for each of the five operations supported by the GUI. In each situation verify that the text display area gives the correct, expected status information and in the proper order.

You may wish to organize your test cases in tabular form as illustrated in earlier labs.

ANSWERS TO THE PRELAB PRACTICE QUIZ

1. JFrame

2. JLabel

3. Layout manager

4. Panel

5. Text fields and text areas

6. `Container contentPane = w.getContentPane( );`

7. `import java.awt.*;`

8 . A borderLayout manager places components into the five regions BorderLayout.North, BorderLayout.South, BorderLayout.East, BorderLayout.West, and BorderLayout.Center. The five regions are arranged as follows:

BorderLayout. North		
BorderLayoutWest	BorderLayout. Center	BorderLayout. East
BorderLayout. South		

9. `double s =Double.parseDouble("3.14159");`

OVERVIEW

In this laboratory exercise, you will review concepts from Chapters 9 and 12 and apply new concepts learned in Chapter 14. In particular, you will take the memoGUI with menu program from Chapter 14 and add another menu item. The menu item will be a typing test for the user. You will need to develop a more complex actionListener. In fact, you will need to nest actionListeners! The typing test will require you to count the number of words typed by the user in a minute and to implement a timer to compute the user's typing speed. You will use the StringTokenizer class from the File I/O chapter, 9, to count the words. For the timing function, you will use the Timer class in javax.swing.Timer (described on http://www.java.sun.com).

This is a more complex exercise, and your instructor may ask you to read this over and start part of this work before the actual laboratory time. Alternatively, the lab instructor may allow you to work in pairs or teams.

OBJECTIVES

Write Java programs to become familiar with and learn about how to

- Use the StringTokenizer in a new setting.
- Develop more complicated action listeners.
- Find Java documentation at the Sun site and use it.
- Use a Timer object in an event driven program.
- Integrate all of the above to add a more complicated menu item to an existing menu.

TEXT REFERENCE

This laboratory assumes working knowledge of Chapters 9, 12, and 14. Key concepts are the StringTokenizer from Chapter 9, ActionListener interface, actionPerformed methods, Layout Managers, and in particular the BorderLayout manager.

PRELAB PRACTICE QUIZ

In each sentence, fill in the blanks with appropriate answers or supply the request information in the space provided.

1. What is the difference between a text field (Jtextfield) and a text area (JtextArea)?

   _____

2. If you have a text field called theText and the following code is is executed

   ```
   theText.setText("Memo 1 saved");
   ```

   then theText now contains the String "Memo 1 saved". Write a line of code to clear the field so that is is blank.

   _____

3. Numbers have to be assigned to JTextField objects as String values. Write an expression to convert the integer value 60 to the String "60" and include it in an assignment statement that stores the String in a variable s of type String.

   _____

4. What are the steps necessary to add a graphical component such as a JButton to an object of class JFrame?

   _____

5. In the laboratory, you will implement a timer object from the class called javax.swing.Timer object to a certain sequence of events. Go and read about it at http://java.sun.com/j2se/1.4.2/docs/api/ and then answer this question:

   What two parameters does the constructor for the timer require?

   ```
   new Timer(delay, taskPerformer).start();
   ```

   _____

6. In this code below

   ```
   JmenuItem selection1;
   selection1 = new JMenuItem("National Accounts");
   ```

   what becomes of the string "National Accounts"?

7. When you click on a menu item sometimes you need to disable the item while its function is being performed. You will need to do this in the exercise for this lab. Go to http://java.sun.com/j2se/1.4.2/docs/api/ and find a method of JMenuItem that enables or disables the menu item.

   What is the name of this method?   _____

   What parameters does it require?   _____

   What is its return type?   _____

PROGRAMMING EXERCISES

Study the memo iconDemo.java program. Note especially its use of BorderLayout.

In this lab, you will use the preceding program and other classes in the directory from source code in your book to add additional functionality. In particular you will make a words-per-minute (wpm) test. You will add

- Add a new JMenuItem for the Typing Test; imitate the pattern the author has established for other menu items; anticipate that the code needed for starting the test will be in the private member function startTypingTest().

- To accommodate the need to display the timer as the test is being run, we need to appropriate some of the screen realestate managed by BorderLayout; add a JLabel to the NORTH section of the BorderLayout.

- The strategy for dealing with the private member function startTypingTest (mentioned previously) is twofold. First, startTypingTest needs to instantiate a javax.swing.Timer object to provide the sequence of events that will happen in real time. This is the basic mechanism for computing a person's typing speed. The second thing is that startTypingTest needs to connect the timer to and ActionListener (as an inner class) that will be able to process the timer events. Use a timer delay of 1000 milliseconds.

- To define the actionListener to process the timer event that will be set to occur every second we need to keep two counters; each will be incremented or decremented on each timer event:

  - There is a countdown timer that notifies the user when to start typing. Use the control-G character (written as a character constant: '\007'), which causes a bell to ring, to alert the user to start typing in the text field.

  - There is a second timer to count up to 60 at which point a bell should ring again to tell the user to stop typing.

  - Finally, after the count up timer has expired, you need to take the characters that were typed in by the user (the contents of the JTextArea) and count the number of words. Use StringTokenizer from Chapter 9 page 563 to count the number of words in the text field.

  - The JLabel that occupies the North section of the BorderLayout is a convenient place to show the count down timer and the final words per minute.

Here are a couple of additional things to be aware of:

1. If you don't enable or disable the JMenuItem for the "Typing Test", the user, if perverse enough, can attempt to start a new test before a test that is currently in progress is complete. (Question: What would happen to your program?) The setEnabled() method on a JMenuItem will allow you to control whether or not the menu item is grayed out. Suggestion: Disable the Typing Test menu item at the same time that you start the timer; and re-enable it when the test is complete.

2. When changing the layout of a graphical user interface, sometimes it is necessary to force the system to redisplay all of the visible graphical elements. This can be done using the show() method. You may need to do this when the Typing Test menu item has been selected.

Testing Program Behavior

Test your program for faulty behavior. Here is a start.

Test Case #	Activity	Expected Result	Observed Result of Test
1	Run program. Access menu select "Typing Test". Take the test.	First timer counts down from 5 displaying the count. Bell rings. Second timer counts up to 60 while you type in the memo text field. When count reaches 60, bell rings and your wpm is displayed.	
#2	Same as # 1 only first type a memo, save it and then repeat #1.		
#3			
#4			
#5			

Screen Shot of Program Behavior

The following is a sample of how the program should respond to various inputs. Your job is to write a program that does this.

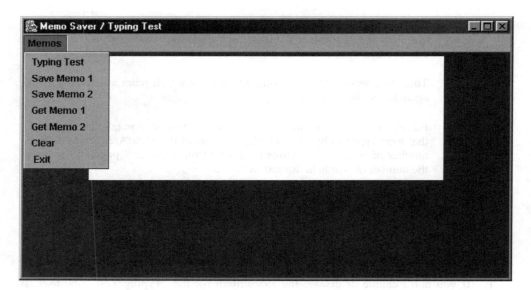

This shot shows the new menu.

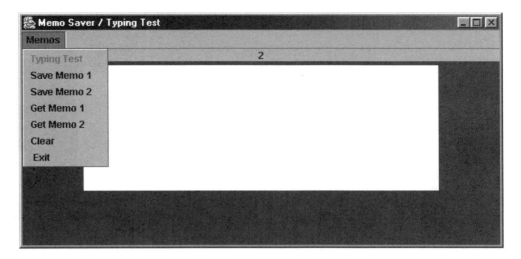

The menu is accessed while the typing test is in progress (the count down timer is at 1 second to go and the bell is about to ring to start the test). Note that the Typing Test menu item is grayed out, indicating that this item is disabled from use while the test is in progress.

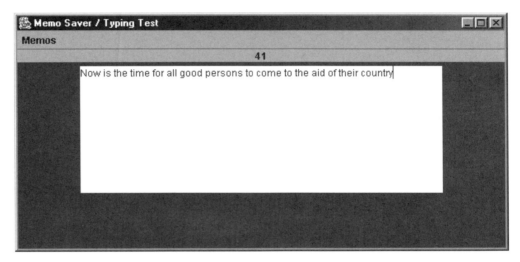

The shot above shows the typing test in progress and the timer has counted down from 60 to 41.

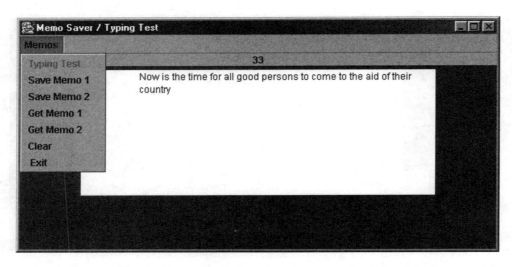

This shot shows another typing test at a later time in progress and the timer has counted down from 60 to 33. Note also the disabled menu item for the typing test.

ANSWERS TO THE PRELAB PRACTICE QUIZ

1. A text field can display only one line. Atext area can display more than one line of text.

2.  ```
    theText.setText("");
    ```

3.  ```
    String s = Integer.toString(60);
    ```

4. Use the method getContentPane to produce the content pane of the object and then use the add method with the content pane.

5. An integer representing time in milliseconds and an ActionListener object

Some additional details that you should read about are at
http://java.sun.com/j2se/1.4.2/docs/api/:

public class Timer
extends *Object*
implements *Serializable*

Fires one or more action events after a specified delay. For example, an animation object can use a Timer as the trigger for drawing its frames.
Setting up a timer involves creating a Timer object, registering one or more action listeners on it, and starting the timer using the start method. For example, the following code creates and starts a timer that fires an action event once per second (as specified by the first argument to the Timer constructor). The second argument to the Timer constructor specifies a listener to receive the timer's action events.

```
int delay = 1000; //milliseconds
ActionListener taskPerformer = new ActionListener() {
    public void actionPerformed(ActionEvent evt) {
        //...Perform a task...
    }
};
new Timer(delay, taskPerformer).start();
```

Each Timer has one or more action listeners and a *delay* (the time between action events). When *delay* milliseconds have passed, the Timer fires an action event to its listeners. By default, this cycle repeats until the stop method is called. If you want the timer to fire only once, invoke setRepeats(false) on the timer. To make the delay before the first action event different from the delay between events, use the setInitialDelay method.

6. It becomes the label on the menuItem on the menu.

7. setEnabled, boolean, void